Depression - my personal journey

Donald Hedges

Donald Hedges © 2024

Contents

But what is depression and what does it feel like?

In this book you will come across many different interpretations of depression; a lot of these will have been put together from my experience. But what is it like? What is it like to actually suffer from depression? Well, it's like being in a really bad mood but most of the time and one cannot shake it off at all. It's like being under the biggest raincloud. What it is I would describe as a deficit of mood.

One is in a bad mood that one cannot understand. The tiniest thing is irritating; people to whom you were amenable yesterday suddenly become sworn enemies, or people to be avoided. Things that were pleasurable in the past become chores, or activities to be avoided. One tends to get stuck in bed, or indoors and little pleasure is obtained from anything.

Often this can start from a singular upset but very quickly becomes a prolonged experience. The effects of depression range from misinterpreting what people say, to sleep deprivation, bad dreams, to food abuse (either not eating anything or eating too much). Little exercise can also be part of the problem, the person who is suffering from depression preferring to stay indoors.

I have given examples in this book but one of the worst things that gave me depression recently was being rejected by someone whom I thought of as a friend; it turns out that she was "got at" by people who said they were her friends. They told her stories

3

which would have been better off in the primary school playground; they told her I was in love with her. I had never told her any such thing, so where they had obtained this information from, goodness only knows. So, she was forced to tell me that she could not return my feelings, when I had not told her I had any feelings.

That led me to be very greatly upset, unnecessarily so, looked at from this distance. It certainly did not enhance my feelings towards her, or anybody else that I thought had been involved in this particular "incident". I know her friends thought that they were helping her but it's not always a good idea to help friends in such matters. Anyway, it really annoyed me and upset me for a long time afterwards. Eventually my mood was so bad and dark that I decided to go back on the anti-depressants which had been described for me and luckily, they did improve things for me. It brought my mood back up to a level wherein I no longer think of this particular person in terms of how I suffered before and it has improved now to the level where we can both be comfortable with each other once more.

Getting in these sorts of moods is not conducive to one's overall health, especially if one is prone to depression. In fact it can be fairly deadly if one is prone to depression. It continues the vicious spiral and cycle of that illness.

Depression as I have stated is a mood which is close to the feelings; it is not the feelings themselves. In my case, the feeling would have been that I was fond of this, or that, person and having one's feelings dashed (having no method of coping with it). That's another facet of depression, one cannot cope with one's negative feelings and experiences. I wish someone had taught me how to cope with such negative experiences in life, it would have been so very useful.

I find myself with no method of coping with depression and as I have previously stated I was never taught any; all I knew was that I was alone and very alone at that and that no-one would come and help me. These feelings are very dark and when one is a child, they are extremely frightening. How come I was alone? I think I have expressed in some of the books I have written the fact that I was an only child for the first ten years of my life until my sister CH came along. Then two brothers, AH and LWH. The youngest of these is fully 15 years behind me and fortunately is still at work, whereas I have retired.

My sister has also retired; she would be exactly 64 years of age by now. Nonetheless, I remember before she was born laying awake in my room, which was next to my parents. I could hear them chatting away downstairs in the kitchen but I could never join in; it was as if I was estranged from them even though they were in the same house. Needless to say that led to me having lots of strange feelings, not least of which was alienation. I didn't have anyone to talk to; small wonder that I began to suffer from suicidal ideation when I was about six or seven. I really began to feel unwanted. That's when I began to take long journeys away from home on my own; I did not like being so alienated.

I would have been about eight or nine when I began to go to Chimes Corner next door to Streatham Bus Garage (as it was then) and purchasing "Red Rovers", an all red bus pass which would take one over the whole network. I began to make very long journeys, mostly into Central London and then via Central London. I could get as far up as Hendon Central on a Sunday. Later on, when I started to use the tube (which it did not take me long to discover) I made very long journeys up into High Barnet, Cockfosters and one journey which I have written about in my London Travelogue to Aylesbury. That costs me about two weeks' pocket money but was well worth it because I went on the Metropolitan Line hauled by one of those electric locomotives (see London Transport Museum, Covent Garden) that were named "Sarah Siddons" or some such. The journey itself is revealed in Travelogue – London and the South East.

In fact the public transport system in this country does have some kind of reputation for being a home for the lonely and dispossessed and it is not unusual to see homeless people riding around all day on the London bus network to keep out of the cold; it is not such an odd phenomenon as one might think. So to run out on one's cruel parents and spend all day riding about on the public transport system is not as odd as people might think and I guarantee that there are kids out there who are still doing that thing, as I did.

So I learned an awful lot about the outside, what was outside my parents' house; I could have talked for hours on what I had seen but they just did not seem interested and sadly, not many others did at my primary school, either. I had a very expansive knowledge of London and its transport system by the time I was about 12; I would go bus spotting. I would get on my bike and go to Park Royal Vehicles and have a look at what new vehicles had been produced before they had ever hit the road. But still no-one to talk to. Until my sister was born and even then we did not start talking together until she was old enough to understand what I was talking about.

In actual fact, my parents were frightfully weird about me talking to my sister, even when she got older; they would interfere and get frightfully protective of her; they would ask her what was I talking about to her as if talking to one's sister was a terrible sin or something which I should not be doing. In fact I was probably talking about my parents and the fact that they were eavesdropping on us was out of guilt because they knew they were failures. Or, they both knew they could have done better by us.

They were overly controlling; what made me sad was that they made things up – this did nothing to aid my depression. I was told that I had used my baby grand piano as an ash tray and it was taken away. They did not tell me the truth that Dad had sold things under me to other people. He would just take things that I had bought and paid for and put them in his second-hand shop and sell them.

He did that with my piano and with my hi-fi system, my desk and my desk chair and many other things. He thought it was his perfect right to do whatever he wanted with all my things. This led to a lot of really strange behaviour on my part; nowadays I am frightened to buy anything new in case it is taken away and I am left with nothing. I badly need a new lappy and I have seen one in Currys down in West Quay; however for some reason I am scared to buy it. I know I will have to but the fear that my parents left me with was that I would have no money, or maybe no home.

That last thing did once happen; they moved while I was still at teacher training, so I really did not have a home when I got thrown out of Chichester Uni. That was the worst thing ever and led to an awful lot of mistrust of my parents and other people into the bargain.

I have detailed a lot of my misfortunes and if you, dear reader, have had the patience to read this far, then I am very sure you will have recalled your own "bad patches" where you must have thought whether things will go round one way, or whether they will go the other. But the very worst thing about depression is that feeling of being alone, of being solitary, of having no-one. That was my start to depression.

I think the other thing that I might note about my own depression was that of the "fait accompli"; that's one of things that my parents had up their sleeves. It's also something that the teachers and educators had up their sleeves in those much unenlightened times in which I did my growing up.

Depression can sometimes mean that one is not left with choices, so one will have to do the best one can with whatever is to hand. I found that when I left teacher training college. This was the first time out of many that I had discovered that I was homeless. They had taken everything from their property in Streatham Common where I had lived with them for 24 years and had transferred to Thornton Heath. I remember my Mum making jokes about that kind of thing, about people moving and not leaving any forwarding address. But Mum, it just is not funny; that is exactly what you have done to me.

I had a lot of friends at teacher training college; they were all gone, only one or two remained. The principals at that place could not have cared less. I am afraid to say that I thought that was deeply wrong because not only did I not have a place at teacher training college but now I did not have a place to live either, which caused me to have a nervous breakdown somewhere or the other down the track. I will explain all this later on. There were no such things as welfare officers or residential officers at college to put you into accommodation during the vacations, or to help you out when you got sent down, as I did. I know that's a very Oxford expression, I believe they also call it "being rusticated". That's a very old-fashioned phrase for being suspended with some sort of amorphous right to be re-admitted at some stage in the future.

What I do have to say is that depression puts you into a mood and it puts you into a cycle, which seems positively endless, so that you come out of the other side feeling that "you" are not "you" after all but some strange creature who is in a bad mood all the time and who experiences no joy whatsoever in life and normal living. Who this person, is or may be, I am sure, is a question which many depressives will be asking and not finding effective answers to that question. That leads me conveniently on to the next chapter which is an overall view of depression and how it can interfere with a real clarity about who we are and one's abilities to lead a meaningful life.

I still have dreams about having a room to live in and sleep in and then it is taken away from me; I had one only a couple of hours ago on this very theme and then getting angry with my father. In the dream he had given my room to someone else and when I went into it, it was not the same and was laid out differently. Somehow those times when I had been made homeless had become permanently lodged in my brain and were still exerting an effect years later. Being homeless is no fun, whatever age you are. They should have considered that at my teacher training college before expelling me and lots of others. I also know exactly why I was suspended because I had an affair with a married lady on the administrative staff which is something all the male teachers there would have wanted to do. They were happy to be putative adulterers; I on the other hand was married to nobody.

Depression – an overall view.

To me, depression means being partially removed from who I really am; in other words, not being aware of the real person and the real things that person has done. This can be a very real problem and a stumbling block to getting on with one's life. It could mean that one does not own or is detached from, one's very real abilities and is stumbling around in a form of imposter syndrome. It could be (as in my case) believing the lies that one has been told from an early age, that de facto one is no good and that one will never amount to any good. As I explained in the previous chapter, one is stumbling around in a cycle of confusion and ignorance, often not caused by oneself. One is de facto in a bad mood. One is in a deficit which has not really been caused by oneself. I have just experienced a really excellent homily in which the priest related a village fete. He went on to say that one man bought 5 litres of water instead of 5 litres of wine to pour into the barrel.

When the man in charge of dispensing the wine opened the barrel all he found was water. In fact everybody had been that one man who thought he would just bring 5 litres of water. Sometimes I think that my parents and my teachers were the people who were bringing 5 litres of water to my celebration.

In my experience, I have never really believed in my own abilities, even though I have been constantly told by people around me especially since I have been a catholic, that I am very much loved. I have had many honours since being in the church, including being in the Guild of Altar Servers and being in the Knights of St Columba and probably to be an officer within my section of that organisation next year.

But the major problem is that my parents (the only people that really matter) didn't tell me that; they would tell other people but they would not tell me directly. That is the way that they created a deficit which I carry around with me to this day. I wonder what they would make of the fact that both me and my brother (LWH) are published authors. They would probably not believe it, or make light of it. They were not used to success; they did not come from that particular orbit. There were other parts of my family who experienced success but I think my Mum and Dad found it particularly hard to measure whether they had been a success or not.

I didn't have understanding parents; their view of the world was pretty jaundiced, even though at the end of the day, they themselves had achieved everything they had wanted and had ended up in a splendid pied-a-terre in Torremeulle, which is in Southern Spain. I have already explained something of my early life with them in the previous chapter. But they still did not know for certain whether or not they had been a success. Maybe compared with his sister, my Dad had not been a success. She had a fabulous house in Tattenham Corner near the racecourse; he had only a Victorian terrace house in Streatham Common with a skylight that leaked and four kids. They only had two kids and therefore a lot more space.

My Mother died in 2009, she was not a well woman and had a recurrence of the cancer that beset her in her 20's. She died at the age of 84. My Dad died at the age of 96, about 4 years ago; he was still not happy, even though he must have had a six figure sum in the bank before he died. He believed very much in money. His sine qua non was that you were never alone with a "tenner in your back pocket!" The only problem with Dad was that all his tenners in his back pocket would go to the breweries. They had more tenners in their back pockets than all of us put together.

Before he passed on, Dad used to go on about my Catholicism; he wondered why I had joined the Roman church. I told him it was because it was the whole thing to me, that the RC church did things properly and they believed in the kind of things in which I wanted to believe; they did a proper liturgy and the way the Eucharist was conducted meant a lot to me.

All these things still mean a lot to me. I did not like the way the Church of England did business; it seemed to me that they did not believe in the real presence of Christ in the Eucharist, that to them, communion was an event whereby Christ was round and about but that one did not actually consume his body and drink his blood. That is what Catholics believe in any event.

Dad tried to say to me that he and Mum had got me baptized and why wasn't that good enough; I did not explain to him that confirmation as a Catholic seals the deal, it does what babies cannot do, it confirms the acceptance of their faith in Christ, the Father, the Son and the Holy Spirit.
This particular form that my father used on me is what I call the "Look what we have done for you!" syndrome. It is designed to make you feel guilty and grateful for what little you have got. Getting me baptised into the Church of England was a thing, yes it was Dad but it was the Catholic Church where I ended up and made that church my home.

That was not the only argument that I had with my father which contributed to my rift with him. I found him very awkward to deal with over the matter of my education also. He used to say "when you get your levels"; there was a problem there because he did not know what levels were. This went on round and about the age of sixteen on my part. I did not have any encouragement to really go on and do O and A Levels. He never took any real interest in my schooling. Levels was probably something that he had read in the Daily Mail or Daily Express. Certainly it used to embarrass me that I had to take my parents to the Open Evenings at school because I know that the headmaster would pass us by and sure enough I was with them on one such evening and he walked right past us in the corridor.

Dad's ignorance of levels was because he himself had not moved up the ladder; how could he? He left school at 15 and went into the Merchant Service at the beginning of the war and was torpedoed twice by the German subs. So he had no real knowledge of what education was really about. That was a deep shame because my Dad was quite intellectual when put to the test; he was quite erudite about politics and had met quite a few important people when he was serving on the Queen Mary and the Queen Elizabeth. Dad was one of those people who were street-wise, that is the phrase which comes to mind. He may have been that but certainly he was not educated and I never remember him discussing my schooling with me. Neither did he discuss education as a concept, whereas I have always been desperate to know where education is all going and whether or not it is improving.

After his merchant service ended in 1948, he spent about 25 years as a second hand furniture dealer. Later on he became a director of an interior design and furnishing company, he was quite good at all that stuff as I recall; his company refurbished the British Steel Head office at Redcar.

Nonetheless, I could not have gone to Dad with any of my achievements, he would not have understood;

that was because of the lack of his own educational attainments. As I said in previous pages of this book, the fact that both my brother and I have published books would have been an alien concept to them, they would have said "How did they do that?" or "What did we do to produce two such boys who could publish their own books?"

I think my Mum understood more about education than Dad did; she was quite well read and she could sing and performed in Gilbert and Sullivan operettas; she encouraged me to play the piano and I got up to grade 7 standard with that. I think she understood the need for me to get school finishing examinations more than Dad did; he probably thought that I would have left school at 15 like he did, I often thought about that but by the time I had got there, the system had upped the leaving age to 16 in any case. If I don't miss my guess I think that on more than one occasion Dad called her a "social climber". She would have liked to have been upwardly mobile if she could have been. Certainly she worked in some posh establishments including Conde Naste. She was not out of place there either.

What was depressing about having parents who did not understand very well (I just about include my Mother in that) was we all had a school system that did not understand either, which just wanted to push you through and out the other side; this was the opposite of any theories posited by psychoanalysts about "self-actualisation". The point was that the teachers were so brow-beaten themselves and so pressured; how could they have got any favourable results, even though some of them did. However, a lot of them just brought a lot of water to the feast, rather than wine. There was no such thing as Ofsted in those days and no-one to measure whether the teachers were actually producing anything. It was a world away from some of the colleges that I see around me today In Southampton and Hedge End who believe in giving the kids a really good and rounded education.

I never got a reasonable school report in my 2nd-5th form years; I got a good report in my first year but that was because we were really only an extension of primary school. We were based in Hillbrook Annexe and had the top two floors (this being a school in Tooting).

But in my 2nd year and beyond, my tutor master just would not give me a good report; my school reports were indifferent to me and to any attempt I would have made at learning the subjects which were put before me. I was always good at English but I am afraid my Maths was a total shambles. I gradually began to build up some kudos with Economic and Social History and Geography and got O Levels in those. I got O Levels in English Literature and English Language. Eventually I got an A Level in English (AEB) at grade B.

Most of my teachers always taught me that I would not get anything, so to leave school with the standard 5 Ordinary Levels and 1 A Level and 3 CSE's was quite an interesting result. I also got six grade examinations with the Guildhall School of Music and Drama.

Nonetheless, returning to the elementary question of depression, I am afraid this held me up a considerable amount; it got worse when I was in my early teens. I would go for holidays with my parents when I was 13 and 14 and stay in bed all day; I had a real hatred of my parents at that time. I would go for very long walks to avoid them. I think the basis of what they were doing was okay, however it was only really very basic. They used to put me in a mood which I could not explain to them. I could not tell them it was because of them that I got into a bad temper and a bad mood. I was angry with my Father; I was angry with him then and I am still angry with him now. It hurts me as a Christian to realise that I should be forgiving him (he died 4 years ago) but somehow I just cannot bring myself to do that.

This lack of forgiveness is part of what I call the never-ending spiral of depression; once a thought is in the mind, it tends to get stuck and goes round and round for years. There's no real logical reason why I should hold things that happened years ago against my Father. It's just one of those things. Depression is not logical, depression is a mood that sets in. Perhaps it's an effort on the part of the mind to make sense of the senseless. I think it is.

When I was a child and a young adult, I had a roof over my head and three square meals a day; they gave me a very small allowance every week, I think it was 5 shillings. I got work on a paper round and did Saturday jobs once I got older. I was still resentful towards my parents up until the day I left school and beyond. I felt that both my parents and the school had let me down and that there was no way I had fulfilled my potential. To just have a roof over my head to keep the rain out was not really my idea of absolutely fulfilling my potential.

The other thing that got me when I was in my teens and early 20's was that everyone else seemed to have a girlfriend; they all seemed to be so remarkably normal and one or two of my closest friends had steady girlfriends and were beginning to get married.

My first attempts at that thing were really quite clumsy and to be honest she was quite handy with slapping me, so that relationship only lasted the minimum of time it could, 15 months at most. I felt I should be in love with her but somehow was not. It was not at all like I had read in all the novels and magazines.

I went to a teacher training college at the age of 22. I am ashamed to say that at the time I was probably only "acting out" being in love with the other person and I was so relieved to see the back of her. I don't think that feeling is so unusual, after all, most people would be glad to be rid of someone who had continually slapped them for the whole of their relationship. I did not feel that she should be slapping me round the face the whole time and was therefore glad when I decided to stop- seeing her and make my own way into the world.

All the time I did actually feel that I could have done better, life at that stage was filled with "would" and "should". But sometimes the feeling that one could have done better actually negates what one has actually done and achieved. I look around and see the same sort of thing now with younger people, especially on my council estate in Southampton; they are not achieving anything, I feel that maybe they are going to be a wasted generation.

Most of my feelings of being a waste of space at school and in my teenage years are really based on depression; if you have confused parents and a confused schooling, one is bound to be depressed because one tends to believe that side of the equation rather than what has really achieved. It all becomes a sort of "imposter" syndrome. Imposter is the word I use because I could not believe that I had realistically achieved anything at the end of my teenage years. If you live life in a bad mood all the time, then any results which you do attain are still coloured by that bad mood. All one's attainments are rather clouded over by the negative things that have occurred.

In my case, even though I left school with many examinations including credentials in the piano, it kind of feels as if I did not. No positive affirmation. There was no way of getting that positive affirmation either. I don't think that anyone really knew how to give it. There was only depression and the thought that really I had completely wasted my time with that school and with my indifferent parents.

What educational attainment I did get was really felt by me to be only part of the sausage machine. I was part of the "comprehensive" argument about schools; whether it was a good idea to have multi-ability schools or whether or not it was a good idea to have grammar schools. To have a comprehensive education in my younger days meant that one had failed to step up to the plate at 11 and maybe one would have to put up with the leftovers that the education authority could provide.

They had labelled one as useless at the age of 11. They had labelled one failure at the tender age of 11. Not only that, they also labelled you a failure at the age of 18 when you failed to get into university, at least that was the way it felt to me. As I relate later in this book, I came across one of my contemporaries at the age of 45, by that time I had an Honours Degree but he was still struggling with a basic level of education and had gone back to school again in his forties, bless him.

That chap had been denied even the most basic of chances which luckily enough I had managed to grab for me; I felt really sorry for him, it tugged at my heart strings. There are so many of us that were school leavers in the late 1960's and early 1970's that had really been failed by the system. Even sadder to say was the Inner London Education Authority was supposed to be the most innovative of educational authorities but I did not really see that until I worked for them and saw the effort that they had put into making closed circuit television programmes at the Battersea Educational Television Centre.

Not that hardly any of my cadre at secondary school made it to university, only one or two stand out at this distance and that was IL, he made it to university at Royal Holloway College and later rose to the rank of Deputy Government Chemist. That's one out of 1100 boys at my school, not a very good success rate.

It seems to me that on the overall performance, this system that we have and have had for the past 50 years in education, just is not working; we are still not encouraging children to do their best and giving them the plaudits when they do their best. As I said before in this particular piece I see this time and time again with kids in local schools; they end up totally despondent at the age of 15, when with a half decent educational system we could do well and we could have a brilliant generation, not afraid to face the future. It occurs to me that we should be teaching things that the students need, not things that they will never use again in a lifetime.

I went into WHS in town the other day to have a look at one of their GCSE Mathematics books. Surely enough it was still the same sort of stuff that I was taught years ago; things to do with geometry and algebra. Things that would not be used in the average employment. I am not talking about advanced employments such as becoming a Doctor, or pilot, or things like that but the question I would pose is, which of us would require knowledge of a right angled triangle in our everyday lives after school/university. Or would we ever require knowledge of Pythagoras theorem after we had left school.

For those of you who don't know it, the square on the hypotenuse (longest side) is the sum of the squares on the other two sides; thus in what we call a three, four, five triangle the square of the hypotenuse would be 25. It's odd how that completely sticks in the mind after having learned it 60 years ago. It only works with right angled triangles! Apparently, it's used in constriction, agriculture and navigation. I can see that it would be very useful in calculating the shortest distance between two points using a method of triangulation. So there, I have answered my own question about what use it might be; maybe I should be a teacher.

All these things that are misfortunes at the time of writing could be conquered if we had a half-decent system; also if we had decent housing, decent services, a government that did not want to destroy the whole state and kept on about the "boat people" all the time. We need to build, hospitals, schools, decent housing, we need absolutely first rate teachers and university lecturers; we need a state that is not going to cut back on everything and is constantly talking about keeping taxes down; where is the money to come from if we do not pay our taxes at the appropriate rate. Most of all we need people who are very wealthy to pay their share of taxes and not to avoid them and put the money into offshore trusts.

In my candid opinion, as an overview we must have a system which does not contribute towards the depression which is suffered by all ages; this syndrome often starts in childhood, further develops during the teens and before you know it, you have suffered a whole lifetime of depression, like I have. This system of depression (low mood) gets its start because we are
trying to organize children to do things at school and at home for which they are never likely to find a use in later life. That does not apply to abstract constructs such as Pythagoras but a lot of mathematics and other subjects just are not relevant to working life.

Please let's not keep creating "imposter syndrome" (low mood) in people, that's not the way; the way forward is to give our young people the best breaks that we can in life, let's not repeat the mistakes that cause people to believe that they are worthless. Please let's not put our children into a bad mood with life that lasts a whole lifetime. Thank you Lord. Let's remember out there that our kids are not imposters. I see a great many parents in our church who are really proud of their children and that's the way it should be.

My parent's basic problem was the only things they really understood were things to do with pubs and getting off their heads on booze. No wonder I was in such a dark place for most of my life thereafter.

Imposter syndrome - an exploration of low mood.

If you keep on labelling children as failures, at school and in the outside world, then somehow or the other this becomes a self-fulfilling prophecy, as it did in my case. Or you will create a situation whereby the child grossly over-achieves and then will be told that he or she is vastly overqualified. Either way, this is not right. In any case, I don't quite see how one can be overqualified; the more education and qualifications one has the better. I still apply for teaching jobs at the age of 73. By now I am something of a polymath. I have written and published 33 books; if I did get a teaching job, the students would be getting someone who really knew something about something. Not only that but before I did publish my books, I had been an accountant, an appropriate adult, an FE Lecturer, an altar server, a booking office manager and Revenue Protection Inspector. That's apart from having been a civil servant and a local government officer.

Labelling children as failures, owing to my early life experiences with unsatisfactory parenting and teachers, I have recurring dreams, whereby instead of going to the examinations as I should do, I conveniently miss them, I dream of not going to them and my mind happily floats off somewhere else, at the same time feeling a sense of foreboding that I will feel that I have failed but being happy to fail at the same time. This dream illustrates a syndrome and a kind of confusion in my head. The medical term for this I believe is "Free floating anxiety."

I feel that it is very difficult to unbundle such dreams; in the dream I am happy because I have decided not to go to the examination and free myself up from the burden of either failing or passing, at the same time, there is an amount of terror at having taken the liberty of not going to the examination.

This dream mostly centres around examinations which I would have taken at school, for example, A Level English Literature, whereby my master had already told me that I would not pass "You do not have a cat in hell's chance of passing this" were his remarks, yet I did go to the examination and I did pass it, I remember going to that examination and doing very well. Yet we are creating free floating anxiety in our pupils and our students by putting pressure on them that they might not pass. It's achievement by examination. But supposing the child is too anxious to be able to perform satisfactorily in an examination? What then?

Above and beyond all of that of course is the fact that what appears to be more important is what one is being told. One is being told that one is a failure before one even sits the examination or examinations; one is being told that one is an imposter. So my theory is that if I am being told that I am no good, then I might as well dream of being precisely that one and drift off into happy slumbers and dream of being a failure and not caring at all, not a jot. They put anxiety there by their ill-advised and ill-thought out words which are supposed to spur us on but actually damage us by terrifying us.

The world of irresponsibility is in my dreams; unfortunately I never got to live my dreams in that respect. I went to all my examinations, attended all of them and passed 99.9% of them. Nonetheless I still have free-floating anxiety dreams about not going to the examinations and not giving a damn about them. Nonetheless we have to ask who put those feelings there; they were put there as the result of bad advice from teachers and counsellors who thought they were doing us good by a little bit of "tough love".

The only time I did get to live out my rather depressing fantasies of being an imposter was when I went to teacher training college in 1973-1975, that experience was so horrid that to be honest I was rather glad that I had failed and was asked to leave. That place fed into my low mood more than adequately. They did not understand the students and to be honest with my readers more than one tutor was having an affair with one or others of the students and if there is anything more damaging than that I would really like to know what it would be.

That whole place had a "Heathcliff" atmosphere about it. Yes it was in very beautiful surroundings but it was quite isolated being on former farmland right up at the end of College Lane in Chichester. In winter time it was a pretty horrible place to get to. Whether it is the same now, I have no idea. They had no bus service up there when I was a student (1973-1975). I understand the 500 Stagecoach service passes by there in the modern day.

During that time, the only saving grace was that did get to live the fantasy of finding love and romance and found a beautiful young lady with whom I had a passionate affair, unfortunately she was also a member of college staff and this was regarded with extreme disfavour by the authorities including the whole of the academic board. They would have been better off sorting their own married tutors who were having affairs with the students but that debate is maybe for another time. I realise that I may have mentioned that particular incident at least two or three times in this book. That is because it was such an important lesson in what goes on in this society; it is an example of extreme hypocrisy. They were allowed to have affairs with the students even though a lot of the male tutors were married; I was not married and yet rusticated through having an affair with someone my own age. Palpable hypocrisy which I have just never forgotten to this day, even though the events were 50 years ago.

But I did get to be a failure, thanks to them. The underlying reason for this was because I wanted to change courses. They insisted I did music. I felt that I was better off on the English Literature side of the equation. They set me a lot of work to do in my year off but I didn't do it, too busy having a nervous breakdown and doing temporary work at the same time. I never did get back into teacher training. When I was at the college I had produced a children's book.

They turned their noses up at it, yet I felt it was such an achievement at the age of 23. What would they have made of my present progress I wonder whereby I have produced 33 books and published them.

They would not have wanted me there in any case. That was one time that I was glad to be the imposter. Both my girlfriend and myself at the time pretty much felt that this particular training establishment was akin to being in the black hole of Calcutta. We cheered each other up with our mutual love and to be honest with you, our relationship was the stuff of legend.

During my sojourn at teacher training college I was depressed the whole time (except when I was with my love) and I went to see the college counsellor; his diagnosis was that I was possessed of an Oedipus Complex (taking power of my mother by having an affair with someone who was married, someone I allegedly could not have). I think that man was extremely dangerous. He unwittingly hurt and caused chaos among many students. I notice that he never made any mention of his own tutors having affairs with students, something which I regarded as a complete disgrace. The whole thing really was the most extreme exercise in hypocrisy, to repeat what I have stated already.

My response to that his hypothesis that I had OC was, well you obviously have not met my mother. Nonetheless what he had told me stuck in my mind and caused me to have a nervous breakdown some time later. It's called rumination, what people have said to you (or the bad things they have said to you) stick in the mind forever. I can recall this particular man looking it up in a book, he looked up OC in a book in front of me and stuck me with that particular term.

At that time I can honestly say that I was glad to be the imposter, if what I had experienced there was a teacher training qualification then I am Lord Muck and you must cover me with mud. What was the worth of such a qualification, I wonder?

There again looking back at that experience was just one other way of reminding myself of being a failure, Donald you have been told by the high and mighty of this teacher training college that you have had an affair with someone who is married and thus you are disapproved of by the Academic Board, therefore you are a failure.

But in this instance I was glad to be a failure because I did not approve of that particular place one little bit and in the end was glad to let it all wash over me and get on with my life. At the end of all those shenanigans I was still only 26 years of age. I had been glad to be the imposter and to have been rightly judged as an imposter. I was not fit material to be a teacher, so hurrah for them! I should point out at this juncture that I don't really believe I was an actual imposter, just someone who suffered from low mood and a lot of free-floating anxiety.

It seems to me that a lot of people worry so much about being an imposter; they worry so much about the burdens that are placed upon them by society and the government, about what people should be, they should be this and they should be that and society should have this or that standard and this or that set of standards and morals; in the meantime we are experiencing one of the most corrupt governments that we have ever seen in our beloved country.

Apart from governmental corruption, there is also the aspect of corruption within big business and the attitude of "cutting corners." I refer to particular items like Grenfell and the Post Office Horizon scandal in this respect.

To me, this is the whole crux of the matter; who actually is the imposter around here; when you have a government which is so corrupt and organisations which have deliberately countenanced perjury on such a grand scale? Although the Post Office scandal is not directly caused by the government (because it was mainly to do with the PO and Fujitsiu), to call the little persons imposters is really a bridge too far.

Is there such a thing as imposter syndrome? In my opinion, not if the person has just so many qualifications and work experience, it would be very difficult for them to say that they have not been a success.

In my case I had been a failure at teacher training college; I will admit this but went on later to get two degrees (Honours degree in Accounting BA Solent University 1995) and a BSc Ordinary degree with the Open University in 2012 with Law and Shakespeare Text and Performance AA306 being included. I have had many occupations and I have previously detailed these earlier in this work.

I have also done voluntary work within the catholic church as an altar server and as a sacristan. I am a member of the Knights of St Columba, a fraternal organisation within the Catholic Church. I have many other qualifications apart from the two degrees. I have the usual crop of A and O Levels, CSE's, RSA's and a BTEC AAT qualification (Accounting Technician).

Yet I still have dreams that I have not turned up to take the examinations and I suffer this sort of free floating feeling, what it is to be free and without worry and maybe to lay in bed all day and not go to the examination centre and sit at a desk for three hours.

The only time that I really managed to fulfil that dream was when I was at teacher training college and I was in love and floated away from the main task. So at that time I had a brilliance in my personal life, even though I did not have a brilliance in my academic life? However my main argument about that was that unfortunately I consider that teacher training was not worth it, the game was not worth a candle.

So, in conclusion, no I am not an imposter although I often dream of being one but is not wishing one would be an imposter a kind of wish fulfilment in any case, with so many examinations to take in life and so many duties to perform, is it not so surprising that people just want to drift away and dream of some other way of doing things?

I conclude that imposter syndrome is just a very natural form of escapology. It's a kind of internal process of self-questioning, i.e. what would I be, if I had not been this. Tinker, tailor, soldier, spy? So my last word on it is, there is no such thing as imposter syndrome, the only real imposters are the people that impose unreal values on hard working people and say that they have been fraudulent when they have not.

And there's definitely been a lot of that all down the years. Coupled with an untrustworthy government, that's a real recipe for depression, which is precisely what this work is all about.

Things like the Post Office scandal and the Grenfell fire are a very real recipe for depression because not only is one dealing with the terrible events of disasters at the time, one is dealing with utter obfuscation afterwards, lies, utter lies and then more lies on top of that. All of this is often coupled with the deliberate decision not to pay compensation or the deliberate decision of controlling minds not to own up or take responsibility for what really occurred in these matters.

The foundations of depression - what are the causes?

To be constantly told that one is no good; that is one cause for major depression and it often starts in early life and carries on and on for seemingly ever. Or until in my case, one realises it. Even in my mid 50s my Mum and Dad when they lived in Torremeulle had a friend, or friends who they would complain to about me, he never phones us, he never comes to see us.

They would see me as a bad lot and I would be subject to their complaints. When my Father died we did not invite any such people to his funeral in Leatherhead and I was so glad of that; he died when we were caring for him and when we all went to see him. He did not die in the centre of a storm of bulldust which all these drunken good timers had created for him; they had created a fantasy illusion which they all fed from in Spain. It was all a bit of a sham and I feel that Dad was better away from it when he came back to this country.

His friends were not my family and I often had to remind them of that fact when I was standing in front of them in bars in Torremeulle, my answer was that yes, I am here now, so I have not let my parents down, not that this is any of your business in any case. But the people to whom I refer were heavy drinkers in any case; they were all heavy drinkers and would drag Dad off to the hotel bar every single night, leaving Mum on her own in the flat. They were none of them there when my Dad died. Neither was I to be truthful but my heart was with him when he died as I had only seen him a couple of days previously and I went to see him in the chapel of rest.

In Spain, my Dad's friends were hardly an example of good living; lots of their marriages were in trouble. Despite the fact that the sun shone all day and most of the evening in Southern Spain, they were still unhappy and critical and ultra-right wing. NF of Reform would have been so happy in their company.

I think some of them were still fighting the second world war; I always remember the words of Churchill in this respect "We will fight them on the beaches and on the landing grounds, we will never surrender". I think my

Dad was still fighting the second world war. Depression and austerity and terrible conflict was what he was brought up to in his youth 1924-1939, he joined in with Oswald Mosley and was an admirer of his. I don't think Dad ever quite grasped the extent to which Hitler would attempt to dominate Europe.

Dad was an unhappy chap; he used to drink quite a lot, he found his solace in the bottle or the glass. Mum and I tried our best to get him out of it; eventually he would settle for going for a drink with us rather than going to the public house in Kennington and kicking up the dust long after he should have been home, giving us his company, instead of his mates. Dad was essentially depressed; he did not think that things had worked out for him.

He thought school for me was a waste of time "Get your levels", he used to say (as I have already stated in this book) but he had not any comprehension of what levels really were or what one would have to do to get them. He was not one of those people who had found God either; I never saw him go to church in the whole of the time I ever knew him, except for Auntie's funeral in Dorking some years ago before Dad died.

He had electro-shock therapy a number of times for his depression; there was no such thing as Mirtazapine in those days, nor were there any talking therapies. I don't know how exactly Dad would have done on Mirtazepine in any case; none of these SSRI's are easy and a lot of them cause side-effects. He probably would have stopped taking it and have become worse.

I don't know if EST did him any good, it probably blocked out the memories of Dad for a while but I just don't know whether it could be considered a viable therapy or therapeutic practice. Anyway, the evidence that I have is that he didn't handle depression very well, he couldn't handle being very depressed and he took to the booze as some sort of compensation.

Dad did not have a schooling; he had no concept of academic achievement and did his best to block mine too. He had no concept of university or any other institution such as teacher training. He had no O or A Levels (or what would be GCSEs and A Levels). Whereas I wanted to go on to university after my O and A Levels.

When I was in the 2nd year 6th at Hillcroft (Tooting Bec) I asked him whether he would finance me to go to university but he said no, you will have to go out to work. I think it had been down to Mum anyway that I was allowed to stay on at school into the Sixth Form. In any case, I did not get to pass the UCAS system, I did not have the relevant qualifications and was sadly lacking in mathematical ability at that time.

I really wish that I had had a father who was remotely interested in education, that he could have seen the value of it as I do. So I went to work at the Inner London Education Authority, at County Hall first of all, then Educational Television Centre, then County Hall again until I left in 1973. It surprises me that I managed three years in that clerical officer position but there you are, people did manage to last in jobs in those days. After that I went to teacher training but as I have previously discussed, for some reason I wasn't interested in what that particular institution had to offer. We had a very big falling out in any case and as I have already said many times I was suspended. I am not ashamed of that fact. After gaining two degrees and publishing many books, I am over being told to leave that place.

I think it was my father's attitude and his own battles with depression that really put the block on what I could have achieved at an early age, I am talking here about teens and twenties; I remember talking to people about it in my Saturday job saying that my Father would not treat me right and it was making me very upset. Apparently there was very little anyone could do at the time.

I could not overcome the fact that my Father was so difficult and so sad as a person. Even when he was fading away on his deathbed he was still so right wing, so dissatisfied with life, it seems amazing that I had any love left for him but I still did and was very broken up when he finally departed. One of my brothers stated that Dad had hung around for too long, I look at it this way, 96 years is a very long time to be unhappy and to create unhappiness in your offspring. So Dad, I love you and blame you for my depression all at one and the same time.

I suppose really I loved Dad as the Dad I would have wanted, even if he was not the father that could have ever lived up to my impossibly high standards, that last bit I suppose is a fallacy in that I really just wanted a Dad who was more of a model to me than my Dad ever could have been; was that an impossibility I asked myself?

They say that about 50% of depression is genetically passed on, that's why I have stood a very real chance of becoming majorly depressed during my lifetime and have indeed succumbed to it.

Mother and Father are the first real examples of people in this world that the child has to model themselves on. In my case my Father was always suffering from major depression and it looks as if I followed him. He was the most extreme pessimist, so were a lot of my teachers.

Fortunately, as time went by and I progressed in my secondary education, I was able to see that other children or teenagers had parents that were not like mine, that did not suffer from major depression and this was quite a comforting thought, to establish that not all parents were like mine, or as fed up as mine were. I used to go down to people's Houses in Streatham Vale, my friends had fathers who were well to do. Some of them were directors of local firms. We would all play cards together. Sometimes I wish that I had parents like them, who were charming and social. Mine were most definitely not.

Other sources of depression, probably the fact that a lot of my teachers at secondary school were not of the finest calibre, a lot of them were very highly critical. I just don't know how some of them had got into the profession; some of them had degrees, my English master WT (slug) had a double classics degree from Oxford and there were some Canadian teachers I remember who were obviously pretty well educated, some of them came from very recognised teacher training colleges such as MaJohn.

And then there were some who pretty obviously had not had much teacher training at all, or were emergency trained after the war (which was a two year pretty basic course). But this they all had in common, the fact that they were all pretty strict and a lot of them would resort to the cane to keep discipline. A lot of them were not as concerned about putting stuff into heads and creating an academe as much as tanning your backside if you put a foot wrong. There were many such incidents that I remember at school, far too many to mention and some of them have already been dealt with in my autobiography.

I did begin to feel that I was dealing with mental illness both at home and at school. I would not be at all surprised if someone told me that my music master at school WFS suffered from depression, he constantly used to say "You lot are a real pain in the neck" but from what I saw of it, he was a pain in the neck himself., Perhaps he ought to have had the electro shock therapy that had been so clumsily prescribed for my father.

As far as I am concerned the real sources of my depression were that my aspirations did not match my feelings, or rather, the other way round, I wanted to do well and I always had such great plans for myself but I could not see that the eventual results were what I had intended to do in the first place. I had to battle with all those obstacles as well as do my school work. I also had to keep discipline over my ill-disciplined and over active siblings.

With my relationships and aspirations with the opposite sex, I always viewed the other person as perfect and fell in love with them as the perfect person for me. I don't know whether this is the French in me, or not, my grandmother was French and therefore I am an absolute sucker for romance, every woman I met and went out with was the perfect candidate.

So it did not matter to me how imperfect they all were, I thought they were perfect at the time. You could say that I was an absolutely incurable romantic.

This was bound to be a recipe for disaster because people are not perfect, only Christ is perfect, Christ and the Holy Mother and God himself. But otherwise we are all, how do we say, ever so slightly imperfect.

My first girlfriend who I shall not name here for pretty obvious reasons, was a bit of a disaster, even though I maintained that I was completely in love with her at the time. I spent an awful lot of time trying to persuade her to make love with me, of spending hours kissing and canoodling with her, eventually we did it and this went on for a while until she just decided that she did not want to be "banged" as she so politely put it.

That and the fact that she would slap me round the face with monotonous regularity really was the living end and we broke up after 15 months; she made me cry a lot, I could not understand how someone I had loved could just have been so horrid. Feelings did not coincide with aspirations.

My aspirations were to get married eventually; feelings were constantly dashed and broken however. Nonetheless, it occurs to me in thinking this through that perhaps, just perhaps, I wanted to marry someone "perfect", who knows. I don't mean perfect from an absolute point of view, just perfect for me in that I would fit the woman like a glove and vice versa and we would be happy together.

My first girlfriend and myself just were not a fit and it made me feel very sad and just did not do my depression any good. Nevertheless, I carried on the good fight and began to meet other women in teacher training college. After some initial mishaps I did meet someone in my first year, she was engaged to someone back home and she got friendly with me and agreed to go out and we had a one night stand together.

Later on in the second year I met what was at the time, the love of my life and we were together for about a year or so. She was employed by the teacher training college, she was very beautiful, she got divorced eventually and I still think very fondly of her. As for the rest of my compatriots at teacher training college, they were insanely jealous of my success with this very beautiful person.

The only reason why I let her go was because I felt less than perfect, I just did not feel good enough, I was just starting out on my career whereas she had come from a very middle class background, had been out with some very high profile people and her stepfather had been an oil executive.

So this time my eyes were bigger than my tummy. I hadn't yet done any of the things that I was going to do in life and I hadn't authored any books either, as I have done (now written 18 books and published them).

On top of that relationship failure with someone that I really should have married, I was told by my college counsellor that I had an Oedipus complex, something which I now know to be an absolutely ridiculous thing on his part to have said and this led me to have a nervous breakdown in 1976, which I overcame in about six months and I properly started the world of work again in 1977.

The causes of my depression are many and various. For a start my needs have never really been matched by any accurate delivery of my needs; my parents and I were a complete mismatch, which was an awful shame because I did love them, especially my Dad.

Then, I felt completely undereducated when I left school because I was constantly being told by school and employers that I did not have the right qualifications. After that it was because I was so inexperienced in life that I could not marry the woman with whom, I fell in love at the age of 23 and I was not in the right career for it, in order to provide for her and any future family in the way I would have wanted.

I still think of these early foundations and compare them with what my friends did, most of them got married and had reasonable careers, for me though my career hasn't stopped and these past couple of years have made me start a new career as an author and a writer.

I didn't know what a career really looked like before I got my first Bachelor's degree at the age of 44 and I didn't get any real help to establish a career either. So I had to forge my own career and continue to do so. It was a whole series of mismatches which have got me to where I am today.

Am I the only person who has gone through so many mismatches in life, I sincerely doubt it; it has contributed to my very deep depression, that is what I know. But the question that I would like to ask at the end of this section was, where was the help? I could have stayed at teacher training college, had they seen my true potential.

They chose not to. My parents could have sent me to university; they chose not to. So many mismatch and wasted opportunities; I hope and pray that the same thing does not happen to our youth which will be the next generation of leaders. Yet I fear it will.

Won't be talking to them again

One of the worst habits I ever got into as a result of depression was that I would not talk to the person again. Or I would get into a sullen silence with the person if I came across them. I even did that thing with my all-time college favourite girlfriend, whom I have described so lovingly in this book.

I would have said with some certainty that this is the way that my parents dealt with a crisis; they would turn their backs on it until it went away, or until the other people got really fed up. They did this with friends as well. I only discovered this when I was about 8 or 9 and there was a couple of friends on Norbury Crescent, South London. I had not seen them for quite a while so knocked on their door. They gave me a meal but explained that my Mum and Dad had suddenly stopped being friends with them. They had been "ghosted" by my parents and told that they were not suitable fare any more for my parents exalted standards.

I could not understand this; I felt that they were perfectly nice people. I could not work out why this had happened. They often would not speak to me either; I would wait for an eternity for them to phone me when they were alive and each time they did it I would experience the horror of the original childhood rejections. Eventually it became second nature for me not to talk to people either. It became my form of punishment.

My parents were extremely tight lipped people; they would not discuss things which I regarded as important. My relatives would pass away and there would be no explanation for what had occurred. I remember this with the death of my Great Aunt' that went by without a murmur from my parents. Not only that but I found that this horrible habit was catching and I too would not speak to people either when it was important to speak to them.

I remember especially not even talking to my father when I passed him in the street one day; it must have been while I was at South Thames College in 1986, when he was working at the Arndale Centre there. I must have been pretty cross with him. I have always been pretty cross with him but to ignore him in the street really took the biscuit. I have a lot to learn about relationships and I am not sure whether even now 38 years late I am much ahead of the curve.

Not being talked to and being ignored when one is a child, is a permanent sort of hurt; one is always looking for retribution for some kind of nebulous hurt that happened many years ago. Whatever. They would not talk to me and that was that. It's a family thing anyway. No-one in the family talks to anyone else and that's still the case to this very day. I find it all really neurotic.

I in turn have not spoken to anyone else very frequently for most of my life; sadly carrying on the tradition of my parents. I don't quite know who it is that I have been trying to punish with this sort of behaviour. It's mighty odd. People are always saying how quiet I am and it's now such a habit that when I have a lot to say people think that I am quite unwell.

In the origins of it, as I have said once or twice, I have tried not communicating with people as a form of punishment but now people expect me not to say anything. I often feel that the only person that I have really punished is myself. Fortunately enough I have had a lot to say in my books, so it comes out one way or another.

Looking back on all of it now I wish I had not made that particular choice, not to talk to anyone; it makes for a very lonely life. My present girlfriend says that I am not really that interested in people. I think that's a bit of a cruel analysis. I am interested in people, just that the hurt from times gone by has made me very avoidant of people and it's really just not right. So I am glad that I am examining my part in it now. I am really thinking about it and what has caused it, as part of one possible solution to depression.

I've always been mad I know I've been mad Pink Floyd and madness.

This may seem a bit lame but I can honestly describe this work as the seminal one for those of us who have suffered mental illness. It is the piece de resistance of Floyd's long catalogue of works and has never been beaten, not by them or by any other band.

It's really a piece about the long post war struggle that we had to put our country together after World War II and the chaos that the post war era had brought about. It's a concept album and both sides really contain just one long piece of music. It deals with a lot of themes with which we are all familiar, the concept of lunacy (hence "Dark side of the moon"), the struggle to exist, the struggle to make just an honest living, the struggle to make a few pennies, the struggle to get on.

It was an extremely striking album when it was published in 1973 and to my mind, it has never been bettered. Apart from the obvious things that it illustrates the band were then dealing with the psychosis of the previous band leader, Sid Barrett, you will hear references to his illness on previous vinyls of their band "Careful with that axe Eugene" for instance.

Yes, it is an album about lunacy and its evident right from the very get go when you hear a voice saying

"I've always been mad. I know I've been mad, like the most of us…very hard to explain why you're mad, even if you are not mad". That's an extremely haunting thing to have to hear but also extremely true.

I remember playing this LP at top volume when I was at teacher training college; I used to play it first thing in the morning, I suppose that was to illustrate the incipient and not so incipient lunacy of what I was doing and the system we were all working under at that stage; the country was so desperate for teachers, we all got in with the barest minimum qualifications; the tutors would have been rejects from any other part of life. If you can't teach, teach the teachers was my logical explanation of it.

So somehow it just fitted my mood and it still fits my mood, as it happens I am listening to it on my laptop while I am typing this. In the 1970's the country was still in a desperate state and there was 3 day weeks and power cuts to contend with, no leader seemed to be able to get it right, Heath, Wilson, not a single one of them got it right. The Labour government at the end of the 1970's just couldn't stop the strikes. Eventually at the end of 1979 Thatcher got in and we all know exactly where that led.

The A side of the vinyl is very haunting; I refer especially to the alarm clocks, in the section called Time/Breathe Reprise. One is shocked awake by thousands of alarm clocks and grandfather clocks. The lyrics of course are spot on right.

At the end of the A side there is a sort of primal scream done by Clare H. Torry who uses her very powerful voice as an instrument; I understand that section was completely ad libbed by her and put together out of three takes. It's wonderful. It is a primal scream. It links culturally with the kind of work on primal being done by Arthur Yanov PhD in California, read his book "The Primal Scream" if you can, it's really marvellous.

Before Clare Torry's piece, the immortal words are spoken "I am not frightened of dying, any time will do. Why should I be frightened of dying, there's no reason for it?" But if you can, do listen to the last track on side A with Clare Torry, there's never been anything like it and I doubt whether there ever will be again.

These immortal themes are dealt with very spectacularly by the band, life, death, the struggle, the wish to get it all out by means of a primal scream, it's all there on side A.

But I suppose my favourite track which is on side B has got to be "Money" and the struggle to get it; a struggle which I never won because I just did not know what to do to get it, nor which career to pursue.

For what my money's worth, I should imagine that this is how a great number of people also feel today, what's my career going to be, will I ever have enough money to buy a house, will I have enough money for my kids?

Will I ever have kids, will I find a place to live? All these things are as relevant in 2024 as they were in 1974 a year after this record was released.

And again after the track is finished, those strange voices (lunatic thoughts) come through "Yes I was absolutely in the right", "I didn't know I was really drunk at that time". Things which one constantly hears and sees. Things which one hears and sees at any street, block of flats, or railway station in the land.

Us and Them, another wonderful track on the B side, illustrating what most people are up against when dealing with those of a higher social class or from a higher rank than them. And that frightening line about a "short sharp shock" (the voices) (which we still hear repeated again and again about people WE deem to be in the wrong), whether they are bad drivers or people who are just mis-spending their youth on creating chaos on our streets and in our blocks of flats., Whatever happened to give peace a chance, to quote the famous John Lennon and Yoko Ono.

For the want of the price of tea and a slice, the old man died.

I think about that phrase a lot when I go into Southampton, so many people are sleeping in shop doorways, especially in the summer, okay some of them are professionals (beggars), some will make a lot of money out of it but there are also a lot of genuine homeless among them as well.

The last track is especially poignant, the lunatic is on the grass, got to keep the loonies on the path.

And finally after one more track, the chilling words to exit the piece, there is no dark side of the moon, as a matter of fact, it's all dark.

So therefore being a depressive myself, I really do understand this very important piece of work by Pink Floyd, which is as relevant today as it was in the 1970's when it was first released. And now it is celebrating its 50th birthday. As good as ever.

The reason why I like this album so much is that it's written for the way people feel, it's borne out of experience, they (the Pink Floyd) saw their own band leader go mad, Syd Barrett underwent a psychosis, he literally went mad.

This is not a pleasant thing to see, I well remember when we were all at teacher training college the guy who lived opposite me went into a psychosis and had to be taken out of the college by his parents. This was an awful shame because there were a number of women in my year who were very fond of him and who would have gladly made a relationship with him. I hope and pray that he recovered from his psychosis, I think he did and went back and finished the course.

We all endured a tough time during the 1970's especially the early 1970's and during these times I suffered from major depression, very much like I am doing at the moment.

It seems to me that the treatment for depression however was not suitable for the case, again I would refer to the college counsellor, a man of the cloth and with doctorates in this and that but a man who did a lot of damage to the students with his ill-considered diagnoses and stupid words. Not a suitable man to be a college counsellor.

This album is absolutely compulsory listening for anyone who suffers from any sort of mental illness and what it says to one has never been bettered.

Solutions - treatments

It's really quite difficult to get effective treatment for depression, especially my sort of depression whereby it's mostly been inherited. My father was very depressed for most of his life and I am afraid I have the same thing. So although depression can remit for a number of months and indeed years, it can come back.

In my earlier years, the depression was mostly on the level of the most terrible anxiety about things, I would worry for instance about whether or not I had an Oedipus complex and when I was about 25 or so and was living with friends it got so bad that I had to force myself to go to the doctors surgery in Thornton Heath; when they saw what kind of a state I was in they gave me a sedative (Valium/diazepam) and a GP saw me; they prescribed a month's supply of Valium which could be renewed and I had a series of appointments with a psychiatric registrar. This lasted until late 1976.

Later on in this book I will describe the situations in which I have suffered from OCD (Obsessive compulsive Syndrome); I have had horrible dreams about having hurt people with whom I have been in love. These dreams are a total fake actually; I have never hurt anyone in the whole of my life. I believe such dreams are a result of not having sufficient serotonin with which to function.

By the end of that time (1976) that I have been describing above, I was better able to cope and got a job as a booking clerk with British Rail, I managed to get over it pretty quickly. However there was no real counselling, just a series of very brief interviews with the psychiatric services and a continuing supply of Valium until it was considered by the GP that I did not need it anymore.

It might have been better if they had really spoken to me about what ailed me at the time, I might have been able to tell them that my aspirations just did not match the reality of my life. I had been thrown out of teacher training college for the most ridiculous of reasons, in my honest consideration and I had been badly frightened by lots of people around me who wanted me to stop the affair with the married lady

Something which these days, would be absolutely ignored by everyone around me, no-one would be bothered with that sort of thing. However in those days, it would appear that the world was a very much smaller place.

No-one really went into the circumstances of whether or not I might have had inherited depression and no-one went into the details of the circumstances which led me to have the affair with the married lady, the fact that I was just so unhappy and disgusted with the state of that college and of the idiot way they were teaching things there.

So, that was the system, the Valium was allowed to do its work as a chemical cosh and that was the extent to which the authorities intervened in anxiety/depression.

I did find a better solution when I went to Southampton Institute for my degree in Accounting; I found that they had a much better counselling system and people involved in it than I had found heretofore.

I was in counselling there for three years with the senior counsellor, SW, she must have retired by now but she was a real good friend to me, which is what a counsellor should be and for three years took me through my anger at my parents and my thoughts about being an all-round failure, even though by that stage I was not a failure and was on for an honours degree at the end of my course.

She was able to talk to me all the way through those 50 minute sessions, of which there must have been at least 100 all down the three years and slightly beyond and she gave me the stability to carry on the course without wanting to just bug out and leave. I was still quite angry at my parents after leaving the course and graduating but at least the anger (and the inverse of that, depression) was not as pronounced as it was when I started going to see SW.

The other solution that I found to depression was that for the first time in my life I actually felt that I had achieved something, I began to feel that I was a professional person and not just someone who was wandering around London with no real definable qualifications.

I found that having an honours degree in Accounting was quite a kudos thing because my degree had a lot of modules in it, all of which had to be passed; it was my lynchpin to becoming a professional person at the age of 44. The other thing is that a degree in Accounting is one of the most difficult things to get. Such a shame though that the Post Office Horizon scandal has given accountants such a bad name. If I had been working for the Post Office in their financial section I would have been absolutely horrified.

Sadly, I never got to inviting my parents to my graduation in 1995. I did not feel that they had contributed in any way to what I had achieved. They could have let me stay in the summer of 1993, for instance, they had a spare room and Worthing (which was where they lived) was relatively close to Southampton. They did not and that really considerably exacerbated my depression and my bad feelings towards them. But anyway I made it into the graduate world.

Just a mention of my work with JHP training in 1994 which was a summer holiday job, I worked there for 2-3 months, this was where I met PMcS and I still know him 30 years later; he is a member of my church here in Southampton, we are both of the RC persuasion.

That was one of the things that I found was really useful to get out of depression was to really do something and taking an honours degree in Accounting to bring me up to some kind of professional status was that something.

I am of the frank opinion that a lot of depression can be caused by wastage of human talent, I feel that I wasted my talents for years after being barred by teacher training college, I felt that there was absolutely no way that I would ever get a grant again and it was only after about 16 years in the wilderness that I forced myself to fight, fight.

Fighting for a discretionary grant from Surrey County Council, which they eventually gave in and awarded me in 1992, lots of people thought that I would just never do that but I proved them wrong. Even then I had many battles to stay the course, the problems of accommodation, the problems of having to move back to London in 1993 and stay at a friend's flat, again in 1994 when I moved from the YMCA to a place in Lumsden Avenue Southampton, all these were little battles which I overcame.

So that's part of the treatment, I think, is to really do something which alters your circumstances, if your circumstances don't match your ambitions, then do something to change it; that's because my view is that depression can be caused by a mismatch between circumstances and what a person would want to achieve. However in order to do that, one has to be prepared for a long fight to overcome the blocks to individual progress.

I think I came from a generation that had very low aspirations, we were never really given any careers information at school and the choices before us were university, teacher training, or going for a job. Sadly what I did was to go for any old job but what I found with the Inner London Education Authority was enough stimulation to want to go to teacher training because I had seen a lot of teachers become very successful television directors, thanks to Inner London Education Authority Educational Television Service.

I suppose part of the battle against depression is to have ambition, to want to better oneself. We have got to encourage people to better themselves, we have to do something about the system that puts potential students into many thousands of pounds worth of debt simply because they want a degree.

So that's part of my solution to depression, is for the person to have ambition, to want to come out of the depression and better themselves. But we as a society have got to provide facilities for people to want to better themselves and that would probably include better schooling, more equanimity between the private schools sector and the mainstream and more student grants.

Grants, not loans, should be the watchword. Unfortunately any move towards tertiary education could be thwarted by the fact that we now have NHS waiting lists of 7 million, so the future government would really have to look at that, rather than the question of enhanced student grants and doing away with student loans.

The other big solution of course to depression would be to offer better mental health services within the NHS; there are many good private counsellors out there but within the NHS counselling seems to have been driven towards CBT, cognitive behaviour therapy, which occurs to me as a sort of thought blocking process.

Don't think that think this. Alter your cognition to be positive. Don't catastrophize things. That's all very well but it doesn't always alter the reasons why a person becomes depressed and it doesn't really alter depression arising out of inherited family situations.

To me the best form of counselling is a therapy that involves talking it out over a long period of time and changing the mindset of the person that way.

Certainly I have felt much better since my 3 years in counselling at Southampton Institute. But in the modern era, to just offer six sessions online whereby the therapists don't even know that you are making progress is just a bit silly and ineffectual. You have got to get to a situation whereby people with depression can go to someone and talk about it.

Part of the solution involves taking anti-depressants or SSRIs which over a period of time increase the amount of serotonin within the brain and this will bring on a levelling out of mood; at present, at the time of writing,

I am on mirtazapine because of such a low mood; my depression has been exacerbated because my girlfriend/partner of 20 years has been in a care home for 5 years and I have not been able to be with her.

The difficulty here is that when one's lifetime partner is so ill and in a home, one becomes infatuated with other people, one pursues other women because of the deficit that has been created and of course there are the inevitable knockbacks. One does not so much want someone else to replace the loved one, as just to have company and fulfilment in a close friendship.

This can lead to depression because one's ambitions do not quite meet one's circumstances. In this case antidepressants such as SSR's can bridge the gap and bring on a sense of greater wellbeing.

But overall, the best solution to it would be to have better and more adequate mental health services and far more talking therapies, to talk out one's problems, if one is allowed to do so, is a positive move forward. That and a positive spurt of speed towards improving one's life and achieving something.

Who will solve my trauma?

One of the things which seems to go completely unsolved in any depression is who caused it, in the first place? This is not the case of blaming any one particular person but more a process of finding out who was responsible for the trauma and beginning a process of forgiveness towards them.

It's like the parable that my priest spoke about very recently in church; the question of who it is brought the water to the village fete in order to water down the wine in the barrel. Pretty obviously the one man who was named in the origins of the parable did that but what was not realised was that everyone did that, thinking that someone else would bring the wine. It's always down to someone else what happens, when the reality is that it's very much down to us.

In my case, I do blame my parents for a lot of things; I blame my Father for a lot of upheaval in the home; he was constantly taking things out of the house and replacing them. He would take a stereo that I had built up for myself with hard earned pocket money and money from jobs and then miraculously some time later a stereo would re-appear. It's like someone coming into my flat where I live now and taking my television and putting another one in its place sometime later. There was no concept of ownership where I lived in Streatham, just a process of replacing things which were taken to Dad's second-hand shop in Kennington and mysteriously replaced some time later.

I did not want what was replaced with something else; I wanted what was mine. I look around my flat now in Southampton, everything in it is mine, maybe for the first time in all my life (I am now 73). The television is mine, the bed is mine, the table is mine, the laptop is mine. When I was small and in my teenage years, I did not have that luxury; stuff was being constantly taken away and replaced. We were an adjunct to the shop which Dad ran and I did not like things constantly disappearing and being replaced. It was a traumatic experience because a lot of the stuff that disappeared actually belonged to me. In the flat I have now in Southampton, I have a collection of DVD's and CD's. A lot of them will be available on line but the point is that they belong to me and I like the feeling of something physically belonging to me without Dad coming into the rooms and taking everything to be sold elsewhere.

That thing is really very traumatising. I suppose what was worse than taking all my stuff and selling it was the fact that eventually he sold the house up in Streatham and went to Thornton Heath. That meant that I lost my room. He did it because he made a profit out of it, following the theorem of the £10.00 in the back pocket, of which he made a substantial amount throughout his life. When it came time for him to pass this life, he did not have very many of the "tenner's" of which he often talked. The reason for that was that he was placed in a care home at the end of his life and it cost an enormous amount of cash to sustain his stay there.

The other great trauma which I have mentioned which contributed to my depression was that of losing my place at teacher training; it does not matter a jot academically of course because I now have two bachelor's degrees but it would have been very nice if they had not suspended me. At the time I had lost both my home and my place at college; not a very happy state of affairs for someone who was just 24 years old.

So, these are the two great traumas that I still think about a great deal. The sad thing about it was that the people who caused these traumas were never really accountable.

If I were to start on the process of reconciliation, I would really ask whether the people involved actually knew what they were doing at the time? It's not fun to have one's place at a college ripped away from one, or to lose one's home at one and the same time.

Let's look at what happened at the teacher training college; they suspended me because I made love to the woman with whom they wanted to make love and it was a simple case of that. To which I would have asked the question, exactly how old these people were, five, or forty five? To punish me because of their feelings was a bit ridiculous. With a bit of guidance I could have stayed at that college and gained their ridiculous Certificate of Education!

I don't suppose any of those people are alive anymore; I know that the Principal of the college must have died more than several years ago, he was Emeritus Professor of Education at Leeds University when he died. I don't think he was directly involved in the decision to suspend me and I never blamed him. What was so wrong in those days was that I was suspended over a relationship I had and that was clearly wrong; their sense of morality was clearly skewed. If they had wanted to make love to this particular woman, then they should have done but they did not and they were clearly out of sync in their positions.

What I would like to say is, that I clearly forgive them all for what they did; at this distance it would appear that they did not really know what they were doing. They had only water to bring to the village fete.

I have to now take responsibility for solving my own traumas about my college and about my home; there is no one else that can do it and the people responsible for such trauma, are very sadly dead.

The answer to it would be not to cause trauma in the first place but then the obvious corollary to that would be to show them forgiveness; mostly they were not in a position to know what they would have done and the damage they would have caused. Most of the players involved are deceased in any case.

On SSRI's as a help to combat depression.

SSRI's are often prescribed by doctors and nurse practitioners in this day and age; what they do is to improve serotonin uptake so that a person can function. After a person has been taking them for a while, it would seem that he or she can feel better.

Nonetheless, they do have some very odd side-effects, both when one goes on them and when one comes off them. When I stopped taking mine (mirtazapine 15mg) some weeks or so ago I was so tired and sleep deprived that I could not do anything and would stay indoors and slob about all day. When I went back on them I still felt very tired and on at least one day did not get up until about 10 minutes to 12, still thinking and imagining that it was the early morning. But I must say that it was a depressing sleep.

Coming off mirtazapine I found that I was having the most dreadful nightmares (free flowing anxiety); in those dreams I was supposed to be in charge of something but as usual was messing it up. Well I say "as usual" advisedly because in actuality I do try my best not to mess things up.

Going on to mirtazapine and other SSRI's can make one feel even more depressed and possibly suicidal for a while; I think I just feel a bit tired and sedated having to go back on them. I also feel a bit sad but am hoping to do better as the days and weeks go by. As an update I am finding that things are becoming a little better, things are improving. Some of my dreams are a little happier than the most horrible ones I have had.

All I can think of at the moment, is that it's fairly comforting to have at least some medication to fall back on, so that one is not totally bereft and also it's good to have one's doctors keeping an eye on one during a period of depression.

On snapping out of it.

One of the silliest phrases I have ever heard when related to anxiety and/or depression is that one must snap out of it, this silly army thing of "Pull yourself together man!" Which must have seemed funny in a Monty Python sketch but which is not actually funny at all because the person is not able to pull themselves together. Otherwise they would not be suffering from depression at all.

Depression is a really serious illness; in reality it is the pathology of feeling. One is instructed from an early age to repress one's feelings, or at least I was. I don't recall ever having had that discussion with my parents when I was small. The question of why I had the blues at seven or eight never even arose and I had the most frightening feelings at that age. I had suicidal ideation at that age. Something which I never told to my parents.

The reason for that I have already described in this book. They would not talk to me; they would not take an interest in me, they were addicted to booze and that would be their sine qua non for existence. In fact Dad would not come home from the pub of an evening and this went on for many years, right up into my teens. The youngsters in the family must have felt it too because they would run away from home quite frequently. We would get calls from the police saying they had been found wandering around in their sleepwear in Streatham Vale, trying to get to Africa.

71

My sister got the furthest; she fetched up in Brighton
one afternoon and Dad and I had to go down there
on the Pullman service "Brighton Belle" to get her; we
had a meal and a drink on the way down. We fetched
her from Brighton Police Station and brought her
back home.

All of this was due to the fact that they just did not
talk to us; they were so absorbed with each other.
They did not have a good marriage for many years; I
would wake up sometimes in the same room as them
on holiday and they would be discussing divorce in
the very matter of fact way that adults do, when they
are having an argument. They spoke to each other,
even on the most horrid subjects but would not talk to
me.

I don't think they really knew about children; what
made us tick. They certainly would not have
conversations with me about anything before I was a
teenager. Other than that I was a non-entity to them. I
had this explained by an uncle once who said, when
you were small we (parents and family) did not like
you but now that you are beginning to grow up we
can see that you are actually quite a nice chap. In
other words you do not become (in our world) a real
person until you can come to the pub with us and be
a man.

That's the same sort of garbage as the expression
with which I started this particular piece "Pull yourself
together man!" In other words, I was a blank sheet of
paper to them until I got very much older and could

go to the public house and drink pints with them. By that time I did not feel that I knew them anyway. By that time I was as cynical and as agonised as they had been.

Pulling oneself together means: pulling oneself out of the black hole that parents and teachers have put you into. That is not such an easy task. I am not sure that I ever managed it. Even now I am still on mirtazapine every day. I am on the smaller dose of the three doses I could have but I still need it. What's so frightening is that it is a sedative, which means that if I get very tired one day I can sleep most of the night and into the next day as well. Which can be quite worrying if one has things to do and appointments to get to.

I have often said this but I look at the way our children are treated at church by their parents and I do see a marked differential between them and the way that I was treated. Their achievements are lauded; they seem to do really well at school and some of them do absolutely brilliantly. They have guidance from good parents, whereas in my case and in the case of my brothers and sister we were just left to get on with it.

So, therefore, pulling yourself together was not an option, if one was being constantly ignored. It was a black hole that one was put into and they were not prepared to pull you out of it. In a way depression is a cruel and unusual punishment and in my view it is caused by very bad parenting.

If they had been prepared to talk to me, I am sure I would have had so much to offer them. I am very intelligent and could have conversed with them on a multitude of subjects if they had let me. Instead however I do feel that I was consigned to the dustbin, which was a shame because now my parents have both died and have been dead some time, they cannot see my success. I don't feel as if I have changed one bit. I always feel that I was full of imagination even in my earliest days and bursting to tell parents my story, if they had ever had an opportunity to listen to it, which they pretty obviously did not. I think the major problem there was that they came from a generation whereby children should be seen and not heard and dysfunctionally just carried it on. They did not challenge it at all.

I always remember my Dad's parents having such weird rules; they had a room for best. I think it was their front room; one was not allowed to go into the front room. I don't know why it was for best or what was the meaning of it. I saw that idea replicated in an episode of Judge John Deed; he (Mark Thompson), would not let his kids go into a specific room in his rented house. That really took me back. Anyway the upshot of it was that Jo Mills (the barrister) identified Mark as a control freak and decided not to go with him or marry him.

I don't think Dad dare let me go and see Grandad; that man was so strict and extremely unapproachable. I am not surprised that Dad turned out to be as depressed as he did; both of his brothers also suffered from the most severe mental illness. This I believe was caused by the terrible parenting that they must have all had in that house.

We must learn to challenge all these ideas about mental illness; that somehow depression is something that is "put on" or some sort of pretence on the part of the sufferer. It is not either of those things. It is just a very serious illness which requires an awful lot of understanding on the part of society.

Even now, after all the incidents of depression that we see up and down the country, the mental health services are still the Cinderella services within the NHS. It's almost as if we refuse to understand anything about mental health and how to achieve good mental health and maintain it. This is something that clearly we all need to have a proper and adult conversation about.

Suicide is painless, it brings on many changes

That is the words of the Johnny Mandel song, so beloved of fans of Mash. Of course that just isn't true and whichever way people turn out to want to end their lives, there is an amount of pain which they have to suffer and endure.

Statistics show that it is also the 14th highest reason why people choose to end their lives. It can be the end result of depression and quite a few other reasons; it can be the end result of people no longer wishing to endure a terminal illness and begging and pleading for people to help.

The church's attitude (the RC church) is that this is not the thing to do; that it is against the will of God that such a thing should be done; I shall be discussing my religious beliefs in a further section of this volume.

My experiences of this are that I have suffered a fair amount of suicidal ideation when I was younger; I had parents who did not take very much notice of me; I remember sitting in the cinema in the circle with Mum and thinking, if she doesn't talk to me in a minute, then I will throw myself off the balcony and then that will make her sorry.

Of course I never did that; it wasn't a definite plan, it was just that it was such a drag to have a parent who never really conversed with one. Later on she would say that I never spoke to them and never telephoned them; in other words the responsibility was all mine for parenting them. That's a very confusing situation for a child or adult to be in; one just cannot be expected to be parenting one's own parents.

I was at a very early age when I had suicidal ideation, I must only have been about five years of age; I had it again when I was a teenager, I just hated my Father so much at that stage. Maybe I hated him for passing on his very deep depression, who knows?

Nonetheless I never really had a specific plan to carry it out; they were just thoughts and thankfully they passed, although the depressions never did, they were an ever present part of my life from the age of about 11.

I want to explore some of the things I have seen to do with suicide and attempted suicide. I will start with one of my experiences with a friend.

This friend was someone who was a bit of a scallywag; he moved in with a girl very much younger than him. They lived in a flat in the centre of town (Southampton). One day she just got really fed up with him and just moved out on him and went to stay with someone who was a cook in a local public house; this extremely upset my friend and he rang me one night at about 04.00 in the morning and said that he was self-harming.

So I got on my bike and furiously pedalled down there, luckily it was all mostly downhill so I got there in about 20 minutes from where I live at the top of Southampton. in Bitterne.

I also contacted the police on the way down; I found my friend in a bit of a perilous state, he was self-harming but not doing it very seriously. Before long a police officer turned up and we spent a good hour or two talking my friend down before we concluded that it was safe to leave him.

I went to see his girlfriend at the public house where she worked, not a half mile away from where she lived. They eventually split up, even though they had two kids together and she went to live with someone else; my Lily (partner) had found the girl a lovely house in Winnall and she married and was perfectly happy with her new partner and her house. She would be about 43 years of age at the moment; she was only 19 when my friend moved in with her.

The upshot of this was, that I don't think it was a serious effort at suicide; he had cut himself a few times in the arms but they were horizontal cuts for which I ensured that he had adequate bandaging; he was in pain because the person he thought he loved had deserted him. Later he went on to have other partners, my other friend got married and is now happily settled. I was glad to have been of help.

My other experiences of people actually making an attempt and one of them succeeding was that I was a Revenue Protection Inspector at Southampton Central Station this particular day, I was working the downside barriers, a chap had come through and asked for the Brighton or Victoria train (on the Southern) and someone had directed him on to the central island platform, i.e. platforms 2 and 3.

The next thing we heard was that he had gone in front of a train that was very slowly pulling in. He had gone into the four foot in front of the train. For those of us technically minded, the four foot is the space between the running rails, it's actually 4'8 ¾ .

The next thing we knew was that all hell had broken loose, the police were everywhere on the station and paramedics and fire brigade. I had to tape off platforms 2 and 3 and make sure that no-one got into that area which became a sterile area for an incident, as we would put it in railway parlance.

Then I was required to be back at the downside barriers to ensure that no-one got into the station. That was a difficult ask but I managed to control the significant amount of people that had built up behind the barriers; all I can remember of this was that so many people asked me the same question, "Why can't I come in and catch my train"; this was an extremely difficult thing for me to answer, you can't tell a member of the public that someone has gone under a train because that's information that they just cannot cope with, in my honest opinion.

So you have to tell them that there has been an incident and that the platforms are closed at the present moment. They will have to wait until the incident is cleared. Normally in railway operations there is a window of 2 hours during which staff and fire brigade are expected to clear up the mess (I won't go into this because it's just too horrifying to tell).

In this case, the emergency services managed to pull the man to safety and he was taken off the station to a waiting ambulance, I don't know whether he lost a limb as a result of going in front of that train, I suspect he did. I remember going into the booth for ticket collecting on platform 4 and just blubbing; it was such a shock. It brings me out in tears 17 years later just to think of the lengths that the poor person must have been driven to, in order for him to think about doing that.

The effect of other people's successful attempts at suicide and attempts which end in a life being saved are never far from one's mind, if one has worked on the railways, as I have. Certainly, as I said, 17 years later and still the feelings are present.

The other point that I want to make is that I feel so sad as to how illiterate the public really are when it comes to matters of people being in distress and taking their own lives, or making an attempt. A year or so ago I was on a train from Waterloo, I think it was 444 stock (desiros); the journey had gone quite well and nothing I had not experienced thousands of times, one gets very used to regular journeys.

But at the Winchester stop, the driver was pulling into the platform and all of a sudden the train came to a pretty swift halt, something which I would regard as an emergency stop. In fact I am pretty sure it was a full on application of the emergency brake. I noticed that most of the train was stuck out of the station towards the London area.

Then the Tannoy announcement came "Would the conductor please contact the guard"? I was pretty sure then that it was a suicide. People began to ask what the problem was in my carriage and I told them that someone had gone under the train.

They denied it; but I maintained that it was perfectly true. The upshot of that was that they detrained us all through the very front door of that desiro set and there were staff there blocking the view. Going through the booking hall there were many police coming into the station and also paramedics and fire brigade staff.

What got me when I was passing through the train was that there were entirely innocent people who were still sitting there working on their spreadsheets as if nothing had happened; I asked them to come along with us, as that train would not be moving any further.

Unfortunately and it makes me feel very sad to say this, the suicide attempt was an attempt that had succeeded, the person did in fact die and it was in the papers the next day. I suppose that was the difference between myself and a lot of other passengers in that I somehow knew that there had been a fatality.

I was a bit shaken up, even though I had a full realisation of what had taken place, I got out of the station and caught the number 1 BlueStar bus into Southampton, somehow that all felt a bit safer. They laid on a bus for those other passengers who would have been stuck, those going on to Bournemouth and Weymouth and Southampton and intermediate stations between Southampton and Bournemouth.

I think when one has worked on the railways, as I have (once for three years as Booking Office Manager in a country station) and Revenue Protection Inspector, one expects that from time to time there will be what we in the industry call "incidents", that is a euphemism for people being struck by trains. I suppose I expect it, having experienced it now twice over.

What's to be done about it? Well on the railway system there's an excellent system called the railway chaplaincy in place, a lot of these chaps and ladies are qualified priests and their job is to look after railway staff and the British Transport Police. I have met one or two of them and am in contact with the head of the railway chaplains. They do a splendid job, I have had occasion to meet one of them and talk through my experiences of attempts on the railways and found our chat most helpful.

It can be a very devastating experience for friends and relatives when something like this happens, people become very upset when others lose their lives this way.

So anyway, the railway chaplaincy, doing good work to comfort both staff and passengers alike when things happen on the railways. An excellent welfare system.

If one cannot find a railway chaplain, what then? Well, then there's the Samaritans, which one can call free on 116 123 or email. These are people who will listen to all your problems, so that after a while they are put into perspective. They are based on the biblical Samaritan, the one who tended to an injured man on the road and did not pass by on the other side.

Whomsoever is reading this, if you see someone struggling on the railway network or acting a bit out of the range of what we would call "normal", maybe try to strike up a conversation with them, ask them if they are alright., Maybe ask them if they would like to have a cup of coffee, or if they would like to talk about it.

It's amazing the results of such an encounter; if the person looks as if they are not safe and you feel that you can't talk to them, the give the BT Police a text on #61016 or ring 0800 405040, or if the person looks as if they are in imminent danger, call the emergency services on 999. Above all, let's look after one another out there.

Not letting the other person's thing become your thing. (Towards solutions)

It's my supposition that oftentimes in life we let other people's thing become our thing, how many times have we been out on the roads and some chump has cut in front of us, or given us the vee-sign for doing something that they consider is not to their taste. Letting that become your thing would be to indulge in road rage, to get after them, to shout at them, to cut them up in retaliation, which could end up in something really bad, or could end up in a fatal accident.

This is just one example when we are wont to take on the badness of other people, we seek to teach them a lesson instead of taking one step back and realizing that this is a situation that can't be solved by going after the person. Their bad driving should not become your bad driving; of course the realization of this factoid has taken me about 50 years on the roads. I am still very glad to have a licence after all that time, with zero incidents to my name, apart from the occasional scraped mirror and one speeding ticket which I compensated for by going on a driver awareness course.

This last thought is not entirely to the point; taking on other people's things is I believe the forerunner of depression, one takes on one's parents' attitudes, one learns from them. In my case I had a father who was badly and constantly depressed. I think I learned my depression from him; I acquired it. The only thing I did not learn from him was the booze; he had a heavy drinking habit. Personally, I cannot stand alcohol. I was very lucky there, extremely lucky.

Taking on parental attitudes like I have leads to failure, failure is passed down from generation to generation. I think Dad felt like a failure most of the time, yet amazingly enough he was not, he managed to get a reasonable sized house at the age of 28 where we all lived for about 20 years; he managed to decorate all the rooms, he managed to get me a baby grand piano, he created a fabulous living space for me in that house. He was not a failure; yet he felt he was.

Because that was his thing and he was the only example of parental behaviour that I had, I took on his thing as well and became a lifelong depressive.

I think that where Dad went wrong was that he probably compared himself to others around him; he had a brother in law who was big in the Post Office (Telecoms branch) and who later went on to have a good job in the Ministry of Defence. They had a nice house in North Cheam (near the Woodstock public house) and later on they were able to acquire a fully detached house in Tattenham Corner, that property would be worth more than 1.5 million GBP today.

So poor old Dad was outclassed; yet he fully maintained a good living from his second-hand furniture business at the Oval for 23 years before becoming a director of PA Contracts in Clapham (an interior design and decorating firm, of which I have made mention before). Nonetheless a lot of the time Dad was really unhappy and would make me unhappy talking about "Get your levels"; this was really a mickey take because he had no comprehension of what levels were and had very little uptake on the educational system whatsoever.

Taking on his thing about "levels" made me very unhappy, trying to deal with it, I felt that he was really taking the Michael. When we were introduced to the senior master of Hillcroft EAL for my entrance to that school I remember that he did not take much notice, Mum was the ringleader in that interview. Dad just did not know what questions to ask; it was five years later that Dad and I met up with EAL in a local public house and Dad brought him a drink, on the basis of that I was made a house prefect. So Dad did do me some good after all.

Having parents who were unhappy was a considerable burden; I took on a lot of their misanthropy. I really wished that they were not so miserable. But it did do one thing for me, it made me determined to get out of it and if education was the key to it, then I would do it and put in a considerable amount of effort so that I did get my "levels" as my Dad would have put it.

I do look around my group of friends however, at a much later age and see that a lot of them, especially in my church congregation, are fantastically keen on their kids getting on; some of these kids are going to be doctors, surgeons, accountants, historians, teachers. Sometimes I wish that I too had gone to the catholic church, everyone here seems mad keen on education and encouraging their offspring to go to university.

What's the solution here because part of this chapter heading is "towards solutions". I suppose that part of the answer must be not to let their bag become part of your bag. That's what motivated me to study at school and then improve myself for the rest of my life. I decided that I could not stay as I was when I was a teenager; I couldn't lay in bed all day and feel depressed and hate my parents, I had to get on and find something worthwhile to do and make progress. So I decided I would work at school, whatever my parents were doing, even if they did continue to make deadpan jokes about levels, that could not be helped. I had to get on.

To find such chutzpah in my life, to try to find solutions, was no easy matter, I was not the only child by this time, my sister CH had come along when I was 9 years old and then AH and LWH by the time I was 15. So I had to play my part in looking after them and taking them out for long walks in their pram most weekends, which was quite good because we had plenty of open space near where we lived.

How did I find solutions at school? Well I started picking on the subjects where I could feel an affinity and where the teachers were not that bad and knew something about their subject.

I started with English and English Literature; I knew that I could write and read well and I could also produce a reasonable essay and do comprehension and dictation. So I did that and studied "The Jungle is Neutral", "Henry IV Part One" and "Far from the Madding Crowd"; this last had been turned in a great movie featuring Julie Christie and Terence Stamp a couple of years after I first read it for O Level.

I did a lot of research on Thomas Hardy who wrote that book, I began to enjoy researching. Mum and Dad gave me a second hand typewriter and from that tender age I have been typing ever since.

I also took an interest in Economic and Social History and Geography, the teachers of those subjects were quite good, if a little weird. I got two ordinary level passes at the end of my fifth year and by the time I was in 6(1) I had achieved five passes, I went on to get an A Level as well. That was in English. All of this I have said many times in my Autobiography "In the role of boy". Thus and therefore, education was part of my way out of the depression system and I have continued to educate myself since the early age of 15.

I want to turn to a very painful subject, which is the subject of relationships; I just was not very good at getting a girlfriend when I was younger, I did not consider myself valuable enough to be someone's partner, why I just do not know.

I did tend to absolutely downgrade myself in those days. My first partner, HM, was someone whom I had met at work, in those days we were all very young, 19, or so (in my case just coming up to 21), so we knew lots of girls and where I worked we had made friends with three or four girls at the Shell Centre and they had a disco one or two nights a week in their basement so we would regularly go down there with them and have a good time and a few drinks.

Working in an office down the hall was HM, she was a pretty thing with lovely blue eyes and brown hair. I asked her out on my 21st birthday and I hired the upper room of what was then the "Pill Box" at Westminster Bridge. We spent the entire night kissing each other.

I don't know what the other guests must have thought, hopefully they had a good evening as well. But anyway it did not last. My thing was that I thought I was in love with her; that's my issue really, I tend to find that every woman I meet is the ideal one for me, which of course is absolutely nonsense and makes life very difficult for me because that means that they are taking on my bag.

They didn't ask that I found them the perfect person for me. Some of my potential partners have really only been fantasies and dreams in any case.

What is the solution to that? If I had the solution to "falling in love" then I would be a millionaire by now. Despite that thing I have had a long-time partner for about 21 years, Lily, who sadly is now in a dementia care home in Swanwick, she has been in care now for 6 years. Her mother had also suffered from dementia.

What was good about Lily; well she came along and was totally unexpected, I don't think I was particularly keen on anyone at that time, well I had been in love with someone in the landlord's office but I got very annoyed with that person because they just would not turn up for work on time, so that ended in disaster. But then Lily came along and we went out for about four or five years and it got serious and we've been together ever since. Lily is very easy to be with and she knows me inside out and there's never any pressure. It's really a good love story.

It can be a very depressing experience when you fancy someone and they don't fancy you back, that can be awful, I still get that sometimes when I think that someone (the other person) is so perfect; sometimes I think it's because I am such a nice person that I see the very best in the other person.

But that really is not the same as loving them and having them love you back. It's not a reality; the only reality is when the other person loves you back. Otherwise it's just a bit of a bodge and a mismatch.

I wanted my parents to be perfect, they were not, this was the start of depression. It's something I have had to accept about myself; I just wanted that perfection that is inherent in having good parents. I try to see the good in everyone.

Towards solutions: I know that depression is the most terrible thing; try to improve yourself would be my advice and try to become the better person, even if you have bad parenting, try to make something good come out of it, try and talk to teachers and counsellors, find and establish friendships with good adults who can mentor you.

Try and get yourself an education. Try to have realistic expectations of others. Yes, all these things would form part of my advice to young persons in these very troubled times.

Oh yes and one final thing in this chapter, this is the best advice that I could ever give anyone is, don't make your bag someone else's bag, remember that it is possible to be in love with someone who is completely and utterly oblivious to you and if they are, there's absolutely no way that you can force them to be in love with you. The answer to it is in the words of the song. The answer to it is to respect yourself. That's the answer to a lot of what depression is. Part of the solution to depression is to respect yourself.

Respect yourself

As a reprise to what I have said in the last section, respect yourself, in the words of the song, that's the only thing to do. What you are and what you do (excluding things like being a mass murderer or serial rapist, etc) are between you and God, not between you and others.

That's a very apposite thing to remember, whoever does not love you, God will love you and he is the one that knows you the best. God will always love you. That's a very apposite thing to remember in the pursuit of happiness, there can be no real happiness without a recognition that we are all a part of God and that we are a part of Christ who came upon this earth to save mankind, hence his cruel and savage death on the cross.

He died for us, so that we did not have to do so. By the very same token he was resurrected and ascended into Heaven to show us that there is in fact eternal life and sent down the Holy Spirit on us to make sure that we had something to remember him by, for all eternity. That is what we Catholics believe; that is what Christians believe. So all of that is a very excellent reason to believe and respect ourselves because God, our Father, made us and he honestly does believe in us. Whoever else does not believe in us, God believes in us. That should be a great comfort to everyone.

There's a very important caveat in all of that, however, we have to believe in Him, that he walks with us, or his son Jesus Christ, walks with us. That's the purpose of baptism and confirmation, visible signs that we believe in God, the Father, the Son and the Holy Spirit. That's why I got confirmed, to make sure that I sealed the deal with my maker. In both ceremonies the priest will mark you with the sign of the cross, that is the seal and an indication that it is forever a bond between you and God.

The one very important question that everybody asks about Christianity is why did Christ die for us and the reason is because it was written by God that Christ would do so, it was part of the master plan that God had for his son. It was God's gift to a world that was beset by problems.

Even so, the Romans and Jews could not see who Christ was and they just went along with having him put to death in favour of releasing Barabas, a known felon. Nonetheless, Christ arose from the grave and sent down his holy spirit, so that we would know Him for an eternity. That's something to hang on to every day, if we can.

All this is a very important thing to remember when we are dealing with the topic of depression, that whoever does not love us, Christ loves us and he showed that love through his death on the cross. That is why in a way, we should be so grateful. Ask yourself, who would die for you. No, really ask yourself because it's so important.

There are very few people who would die for you. And that's stating the definite. I think if more people came to the church and believed in Christ, the less depression there would be. In my case my belief in the Almighty makes things a lot less horrid than they would be if I were on my own. I know God loves me; if you have the love of God then it's much easier to respect yourself.

The role of the church in all this (Depression).

I believe that the church (and by that I am talking about all churches in the Christian tradition) has a substantial role to play in helping people avert depression, or even when they have it, to help sustain the people's belief in God as a healing power. That's very important. The role of the church in education cannot be underestimated; I have not taught in a CE or Catholic primary school, or secondary school but I should imagine that they are very good.

Certainly outside the school system and in the church system especially the RC church, the priests are very good. They are very educated and a lot of them give very excellent homilies; that's part of being a seminarian, you are taught there to give really excellent homilies. The church of England would call these "sermons".

My particular priest always tries to bring in his own experience into his homilies, I always enjoy his tales about how he had an uphill struggle to be a priest and most of his own family were against it and put representations to the archbishop of his diocese saying that he should not become a priest.

In my opinion that man is admirably suited to be a priest, a man of God, even he is not suitable, then call me a log and toss me into the fire.

And of course in the catholic tradition, we have the saints, all of whom have been marvellous and have done such beautiful things and not in a self-serving tradition either but have done things for us and have showed us the way when we did not know the way ourselves and here I am talking about even Kings not knowing their way around.

Here I make reference to people like Sir Thomas Moore who was canonised; he just would not give in to the demands of his King, even though everybody else has signed off to say that they supported the king St Thomas Moore just would not do this and was executed for it.

The church (RC and CE) is full of scholars and theologists who constantly make us think, who re-define what is going on and make it more in the image of Christ. We therefore celebrate all these people who have given to the church and whose words are so terribly wise and whose words have the ring of truth in this day and age.

We look up to these people and we admire them very much; I very much doubt if my words will have the same ring of truth all down the ages as those of the very able theologians, catechists and scholars that we have in the church.

Why does this matter and what is the relevance to depression, I hear the readers ask? My answer is that a lot of these scholars are deeply steeped in theology. They have studied what it means to be a believer in Christ; they have actually gone out of their way to show us what the gospels mean and what it means to be in the service of God and Jesus Christ, often in very poor circumstances and not asking for anything.

That's why the church is so important to people in times of illness and by this I include depression because hearing the excellent words of the saints and theologians can bring us relief from suffering; many of them have worked with the sick and suffering like Jesus himself did. So alll in all it's a bit of an inspiration.

I want to go back to what my own parish priest has been through; that must have been a very depressing experience, to have his own archbishop tell him that very many people in his family were against him becoming a
priest; it makes me recall my own struggle with my dying Father "Why do you want to become a catholic".

Well Dad because Christ died for me and so did all the saints and martyrs, that's why I wanted to be confirmed into the church. And anyone who becomes a priest against all that opposition in the family is part of a church of which I can be proud.

I could go on and on about this; suffice it to say that God cares about each and every one of us, therefore respect yourself, whatever the gap between your aspirations and your achievements, remember that

God will never let you down. Respect yourself, just as God respects you. Finally the church is against suicide as I believe it should be. Life is something that is god given and should not be terminated by self-will. That's a very important thing to remember.

Reconciling feelings and aspirations

I believe that a lot of what ails us is feelings not quite meeting reality, or even the reality of one's aspirations. I found that quite a lot in the world of work whereby seemingly I was the proverbial square peg in a round hole. I have been through all this in my writings and I don't propose to tire the reader with this any further. I well remember the words of my headmaster JO in this respect who said "Well you have three choices, work, university or teacher training college." He never said anything about doing something that you love and that you would enjoy doing and which would bring you pleasure all down the ages.

To my way of thinking, that attitude is an awful shame; these people were supposed to be educators, yet in not one classroom did they ever cultivate in one, a love of books, which I find so absolutely essential in someone who is going to become educated. I for one don't do half enough reading; I do a lot of writing out of my own head which does not always require a great deal of research. I do that because I feel I have a lot of experience to offer other people. I suppose I am telling a bit of a fibber about that because in order to have become this educated I must have read an awful lot. I certainly read for both my degrees as one is supposed to do.

I think that in our society we become overly mired in getting people to work and somehow think it is a criminal offense to be in benefits when one cannot get work and when one has to sign on. But life is not all about getting work.

Life to me is about doing things that you enjoy doing and would bring you pleasure. That's where Education comes in. The first stage of this should be getting our children to read and write because it is mainly through reading and writing that one can meet the world. One can take on the experience of older and wiser counsels and one can find this in the world of reading. As one of my tutors used to say "You must go to the library, they are full of books!" Students so often forget that when they are so stuck on going on the internet to find out what is necessary for their assignments. It is necessary to read as well.

Reading is an absolutely essential part of education and it should be something which children are encouraged to do from a very early age.

My love of both reading and writing has brought me great joy, I have been writing books since I was at teacher training college many years ago. Now I have had 18 books published.

I find writing is a very good way of communicating with others. Along with reading and writing of course is the pursuit of ideas and the pursuit of thoughts and reflective thinking and reasoning. All these things are an excellent way of grappling with depression.

They can also be a way of reconciling where you are now and where you would like to be in the future. If you can't be where you would like to be and there is a gap between where you are now and your aspirations, then you can always write about it, which I do all the time. Write your feelings down and keep a life diary or a scratch pad of your life.

Writing it all down is a sort of self-therapy, it's between you and the written word and you can say exactly what you like in your own diary. There is nothing wrong with making plans in your own personal diary either; you can be what you want to be in your own personal diary, that's why I find writing so liberating. If you can't be what you want to be at the present time, then you can be on paper. So write your dreams down, put them into writing. One day they might all come true.

Writing for me and publishing is also the way that I share with the world what might have been but also what can be and it's amazing how many people agree with what I have written. People's experiences are not so vastly different that they cannot be shared.

There is no block on dreams or fantasies in trying to reconcile what you want out of life and it can be a healthy thing as well because a lot of secrets and plans can be revealed in dreaming, as well as in the odd sort of dreams which one has at night-time and when one is napping.

For instance I always have dreams that I have been employed by someone and am trying to achieve something but am simply hopeless at it.
Somehow though the hopelessness always seems to be fun. There is no sadness about not knowing what I am doing. I reconcile this by thinking that these sorts of dreams are partially memories of childhood. One plays in childhood as a way of organising the world and to practice joining the adult world. That is how one learns how to cope with the adult world.

So therefore, plans, dreams and fantasies are good. They help us cope with depression and help us carry on functioning when times are hard for us. They are a bridge to sanity. That's because no one can stop them. As far as I know there is no employer in this world who can stop you daydreaming!

The other positive things one can do to aid depression involve an interaction with the church which is something I have done for the last seven or eight years, the last five of them as an altar server and sacristan.

For me the educational aspects of being associated with the Roman Catholic church have been truly splendid, what I love about the church is that it is so structured as to be wonderful. For example, the liturgy of our church is fully contained in both the Sunday and the weekly missals.

These texts never fail to inspire. The missals are brilliant and always have something to inspire every single day and every single Sunday that one digs into them. So even if one does not study the bible regularly, reading what's in the missal can be of great benefit to one and can be stimulating.

The other great thing is keeping one's faith going, which is always encouraged in the Catholic church. It's always nicer to be in a church and to have a faith than it is to be without it. In addition I have found that being in the Catholic faith has been very comforting to me in times of trouble and depression.

So there it is, the solutions to bridging the gap between aspirations and depression. One can write about it, one can dream and fantasize about it and often these dreams and fantasies can turn out to be plans for the future and one can of course join a good church which has really helped me in my depression.

There are miles of other things which I have not mentioned, all of which will help, such as getting exercise and sports and hobbies. All these things help bridge the gap between depression and aspirations and are healthy.

Fighting childhood battles when an adult. Dreams of long ago

A lot of the things I have described in this book are actually recalls from childhood, that's the thing about depression (and anxiety), they come from one's early times. Remember how I have described in the previous pages of this book, how I have free floating dreams about being employed and then being absolutely hopeless at the job but it being quite fun at the same time.

The same theme occurs when I have dreams about failing my examinations, that again is free floating in that I don't go to the examinations and I am quite happy about it; in fact it's quite fun. I hadn't quite worked it out as far as I have now but it's my own theory and it does seem to fit.

Childhood should be a time of very little responsibility and a lot of fun; unfortunately mine was stolen from me but a lot of responsibility and parents who were extremely misguided. I believe my dreams are an attempt to go back and restore my inner equilibrium.

My lost childhood; is a cause of a lot of my depression, having to be overly responsible for my parents from the age of five was not awfully funny, so when I am asleep at night I dream of trying to do adult things from an child perspective; this was something I had never quite worked out before. In my dreams I am totally hopeless and completely inept and what's even funnier is that I am actually enjoying it.

It's also a compensation for my childhood when I was not allowed to be a child. Free floating dreams are an attempt to get back to that childhood and correct it.

It's my way of correcting it, in any case. It's also my way of connecting back to my childhood and for the first time these things make sense. That's because in my childhood I was never given the chance to be irresponsible; only the opportunity to be completely responsible before I was even ready to be such.

That's really what I want to say in this section; depression can be a way of making sense of the senseless, it's not a feeling in and of itself but it's close to the feelings, in a way depression is a reaction which masks the very painful feelings that are underneath it but I find that if you wait long enough you can make sense of the dreams that you have (of childhood and of growing up).

Childhood should be a fun time and it's this that comes through in my dreams; of course the adult theme of taking examinations and working also comes through as well and the reason for that is that I was forced to be an adult by my overbearing father long before I was ready. But to go to work and be doolally at it as I am in my dreams would be a fun experience.

I have just never tried it unless I have been under extreme pressure. If I have been under extreme pressure then I must admit that I have left one or two jobs; that is the adult counterpart of being "free floating".

Depression and mental health are viewed sometimes as failures. A friend has supplied me with the following information about the Irish attitude towards mental health, which is to say 66% of adults believe that being treated for a mental health difficulty is still seen by Irish society as a sign of personal failure. 21% of Irish adults would consider it a sign of personal weakness if they sought help for a mental health difficulty; that's from a report dated 2021. (Source, MF.)

I have discussed this in terms of failure before and earlier in the book, probably if I said to the doctor that I had free floating anxiety dreams, he would not understand very readily, it's the kind of thing that only really psychoanalysts and psychiatrists understand. But it's my theorem that it's my attempt to put some security back into my childhood where there is none.

It's not only childhood that suffers from an attempt to have it stopped at the hands of overbearing parents; I also found this when I was a teenager; only I was able to get rid of some of the angst by turning my anger against Mum, I was too big to hit by this stage, it wasn't a great amount of anger, just enough to let my parents know that I was there.

What's the solution? If I had been allowed to have a childhood then I probably would not have been in bed last night having free floating fantasies about being in a job that I cannot do? However, having a parent who put on me more than I could cope with started this process.

What's the answer; be a good parent, that's the answer, don't put pressure on your child to solve your problems, unfortunately that's what my parents did. They were not happy with each other for the first 10 years of their marriage and I was the one who got punished. That's not a good idea; it's not the child's fault. But we are talking about the post war era, when it was a time of great struggle in society, in fact I feel that the post war era went on far more than was necessary; they were still fighting the austerity battles in the time of Heath and Wilson in 1973-1974, that's nearly 30 years after World War II ended. That can't be right. We won the war yet we did not win the peace.

The answer to it is please be a good parent if you are going to have children; don't leave them to flounder and don't leave them to depression when they become teenagers, like I was. Attention to the needs of children at the right time can prevent a whole lifetime of depression. Fortunately I do see within my church groups and the congregation in general some very good examples of bringing up children.

 I have already stated how valuable the church is in this respect because all of us, clergy and ministers alike in the RC church want children to have the best start in life and to go on to have the best life. That's just so important, bringing up children properly is just so important. It's vital for our survival as a society.

I am still fighting the good fight with my Father; I am still involved with arguing with him and having to deal with his unpleasantness. I have very unpleasant dreams of him and his challenging behavior and these dreams have not gone away; they have been there all my life. That's because he was just so awkward and so was Mum, come to that. They would find controversy in everything I did and if I ever brought a girlfriend home, that would be even more controversial. I should not have to put up with having bad dreams of Dad, even years after he died.

To have to deal with parents who found controversy in everything I did is extremely boring; I am only so sorry that it took me years to find good Christian people who only want peace and who do not seek for every bit of controversy that they can get their hands on.

Carer's depression

I want to talk about this because I feel it is so important that this topic is included in this book. I have probably stated elsewhere that I was caring for my girlfriend Lily for about 7 years from 2011-2018 and then she went into a home, now presently in a care home in Swanwick with full nursing facilities because unfortunately she broke her hip at a previous residential home and can now no longer weight bear, which is very sad.

I suppose I must have noticed her increasing dependence on me when I was an appropriate adult with Hampshire Police, this would have been in about 2011, I remember having conversations with my supervisors stating that she was becoming more important than the voluntary work.

Throughout the period 2011-2018 Lily got progressively more erratic, until she was trying to start the day at 0400 in the morning, which made me exceedingly cross; she then started losing things at an alarming rate, she lost a big bag of documents one day, which seemed to carry a large part of her past.

 When questioned she denied that these documents and this bag meant anything to her; then she lost her keys. Finally she would not recall or remember that she had her own flat (this being in 2018) and handed herself into the doctor stating that she no longer knew what she was doing.

I had cared for her for 7 years when the denouement occurred, it was bound to happen because I just felt that there was something very wrong with her behaviour, she would get into tempers with me and pretend that she was going to smash one or other bits of my gear up at home; she started having falls, she started clinging on to the front door when I tried to shut it against her; she would hang on to my wrist in anger. All of this was not the gentle person that I knew.

After a whole series of enquiries and an eventual consultation with the psychiatrist at Western Hospital I concluded that something was very wrong; I went to see them on the occasion of Lily being admitted into hospital at Southampton General and was told that yes indeed, they had formulated a diagnosis of Alzheimer's Dementia; that was also the conclusion of the doctors at SGH after they had given her a brain scan.

The sadness of this was that I had been a carer for her for all those years, yet in the final analysis I could not do anything, she was just becoming too unmanageable to be able to look after. Since her diagnosis in 2018, she has been in more than one care home, she has been in Glen Lee (in the same road as myself in Bitterne), then Springfield House in Woolston, where she contracted covid and had to be hospitalized, then Ranvilles in Fareham, Forest Edge in Cadman (the subject of a Guardian article in which Lily and I are both featured), Forest Court in

Tatchbury and finally Hawthorne Court in Sarisbury Green where the old Coldeast Mental Hospital was situated.

Lily was such a bright person before her diagnosis of dementia; I remember that she was extremely good as my learning assistant on my Shakespeare course AA306 in 2011-2012 with the Open University. I owe her a huge debt of gratitude for assisting me on that course because of my disability (diabetes type 2).

Not only that but she's very special to me because she picked me to be her boyfriend, she came and found me, that's the first time in any relationship of mine that anyone has ever done that. She thought I was dead cool and that was in 2003 and we have been together ever since. The sadness of it is though that in a way we are not together anymore because we have been parted by her dreadful illness.

This has led to my depression, or rather contributed to it. One gets used to someone being around; Lily was around for 15 years before she went into the care system and I got so used to her being around that when she and I fell out I really used to miss her.

One gets very used to one's partner. So it's quite a wrench when they get put into care. But she is always glad to see me when I crop up at the nursing home where she is now. I don't really get to see her that much, always busy with the writing and travelling about and also with church functions.

What's the solution here? Well despite it being a very depressing experience to have one's partner going into the care system, there is not much that can be done, except to keep busy. As I said, I keep busy with church functions, I regularly attend mass once or twice a week and serve and keep busy with the sacristan functions, I have taught on the Bible Timeline courses and I attend faith groups regularly. I also travel a lot locally and at weekends up to London and back; mostly my travels are to Portsmouth and back during the week from Hedge End Station and back to Southampton on the fast service (Great Western Railway), that's a nice thing to do during the evenings and it keeps me busy for two to three hours.

I really miss the fact that Lily and I used to go out a lot. We went to Paris together on more than one occasion and she really enjoyed that. I took her to Notre Dame Cathedral in 2016 and we took part in the mass together.

One's partner going into care is the occasion or event of very many big changes in one's life, so it's the beginning of finding a new way of life, for me this has been quite a challenging experience and not one that I had ever thought would be possible; one tends to think that one's partner will be forever. I have found that the answer to it is to keep going as best as you can and to find things to do; with me it has been my writings (I have now published five books on Amazon), my work within the Catholic church and my travels, which have taken me all over the south on buses and trains.

That stops the feeling of being depressed, or makes it more tolerable. One's partner is very difficult to replace, I really do miss the closeness that Lily and I had together and I regret that she now has dementia because it's like I have been robbed of her. She's still there when I go to see her but not there in another sense because of the illness. They do their level best to care for her at Hawthorne Court and for that I am extremely grateful.

I still do what I can to care for her, I attended meetings for her to get continuing nursing care and this was awarded to her last year which means that she gets NHS partial funding for the nursing portion of her stay at HC. I am also her DOLS representative (Deprivation of Liberty Safeguards). In addition when she needs to go to hospital in patient transport I go with her as her chaperone, the last time she went to hospital was to the QA in Cosham for kidney stones. I never did get a notification of how that particular issue had been resolved.

It's very difficult having a partner wrenched away from one, especially in the circumstances I describe, I try my best to keep busy and focused on what I have to do, the pain of it does not get any less, all I try to do is my best (as my paternal grandmother would have said), that's all I can really do in the situation. There is no magic solution to it and I say prayers for all of you who are in the same situation as me and have lost relatives and friends to this dreadful ailment.

Don't keep it hidden. Depression as some kind of shame.

Part of the reason why I have suffered depression so badly all my life is that I have kept it hidden, from most people, from those closest to me and especially from myself. I have always felt that there is some shame in mental illness. Depression is an especially difficult one because it is so difficult to explain why one "feels differently" to other people. It's also difficult to explain why you don't get the normal enjoyment out of life that other people do. Yes, other people "get the blues" but when a depressive really gets the blues then it's really something else because it's a real clinical illness.

I didn't enjoy school for instance, in the way that others would have enjoyed school, apart from the fact that they enjoyed caning us so much and bullying us and making fools of us. I managed to survive to the sixth form and even then I used to spend days on end planning on how I would leave, how I would pack it all in. Fortunately there was so much to do on the prefect front and on the House vice-captain front that I did not get time to feel that down. Just sometimes however it used to grip me and I would just wish that I did not have to do any of it.

I didn't really like being one of the senior masters enforcement army; it was just something that we had to do when we all got to that particular stage of our secondary education. We had to keep the younger ones in order while the teachers sat in their comfortable staff room quaffing tea and biscuits.

I don't know whether any of my friends felt the same way about so many aspects of our secondary school. I don't think they all did well academically though. I have already mentioned my friend JY who was still studying and trying to get some qualifications at the age of 45. I met him at Carshalton College; that would have been 28 years ago now and he would be, like me, 73 years of age. At that time I had been in receipt of my Accounting degree for a year and was happy passing on what I had learned at Southampton Institute.

I do not know whether any of them at school knew how I suffered with depression; I could not take authority, I would rebel against it. I would object to being told what to do by the school captain even though he was a close friend of mine; they mostly let me do what I wanted as a school prefect, so they must have known I did not take authority well. I was allowed to pick and choose whatever duties I wanted to do, luckily. I had my own version in my head of what it was to be a school prefect and would do that, rather than what was laid down. Most of the school prefects would do a set duty. I would do any duty that I picked for myself; why they did not make me a senior prefect I do not know because I would not do what I had rostered for myself and would act like the other senior prefects. I had a roving brief which I had picked for myself.

I have already detailed that some of the teachers used to make my depression and mess me up. I have gone on endlessly about WFS, the music master. It wasn't a true music department, it was only a small thing with him in charge. I just did not like him. Mostly my depression coloured what I felt about teachers, I felt that they were better when I was sitting down having a drink with them in the local pubs, rather than on a business basis.

Still, no-one recognised my illness and I never told anyone about it until 1976 when I was diagnosed with acute anxiety. I suffered throughout teacher training college with depression. I used to get terribly hurt when things did not work out with various women with whom I had friendships and relationships. I used to take break up very hard. Nonetheless the main thing that I remember about the campus there at Chichester was that it was very isolated; there was no college bar at the time, yes, we did have discos and we did college plays at the time but if you wanted a drink you had to go out. Fortunately some of my girlfriends had cars, so that was not so bad.

I found it very hard to explain my point of view to the tutors; I never told them I was depressed or that I found college as a place grindingly harsh, I would miss home terribly. I would long for the vacations when I could go back home and earn money and be in London and go back to my room in Streatham; that seemed more normal than being so isolated. On reflection I should really have gone to work permanently with Granada after my first terms in

Chichester; I should have stayed with them. I liked them; I liked the way that Lord Bernstein would chat to me in the lift when I met him. I liked the way he ran the company; it was a fun place to be.

I did not like, probably as a result of my illness, what I was being taught at teacher training. I would write to the principal about it. My girlfriends would accuse me and sometimes compliment me about being a "one-off", different from a lot of other males. Certainly when I met my married lady, we were both of a similar mind about that place. She called it the "Black hole of Calcutta". I agreed with her.

The point about being depressive is that we feel things differently, we feel things more deeply, I believe. We don't always like what we are being taught and we want to argue with it. I happen to believe that is what makes depressives very inspired people. I hear that Sir Winston Churchill used to suffer from what he called his "black dog". There again he was an extremely inspired man. One can be a depressive and still be extremely productive.

The only place that I have never really had an argument with the authorities is the Catholic church. That is the only place that I have really been obedient. That's because what happens in the church always seems right to me. The other though I have about it, is that you cannot argue with God; He knows all the arguments. There is not a single argument that He would not have heard. I have also not met a single priest that was not inspired and who had utter faith in what they were doing. That's what I like so much about the Catholic church; it's extremely thorough and very principled throughout.

Having said all that, there's nothing shameful about being a depressive. If anything it can lead to one being very creative. Despite my depression, I have managed to produce 18 books on Amazon, I am very active within the Catholic church and am very qualified. I don't know whether I would have done any of these things if I had listened to anyone else though. I have made it a habit not to listen to anyone else throughout my life and I doubt whether I would start now. Unless of course they happen to be in my church; then I will gladly listen to them.

I have long since accepted that my depression is an integral part of me. It is a part of who I am which means that I see things differently from others and it cannot be helped. The only thing of course I wish I could hide is that it does make me feel very mopey at times and it's a bit energy sapping. I try to take my medication regularly so that I am reasonably balanced. There does not seem to be much alternative to anti-depressants at the moment. I wish they would discover something.

My recommendation is that if one suffers from a mental health ailment then one should be able to tell someone about it. Don't do what I did and keep it all hidden. A lot of people are suffering from this ailment and it would be better if it were all released out into the open. That's why I am writing this book and republishing and constantly editing it, so that people can understand what we go through in depression. A little education on this subject would go a very long way.

If anything, it has helped me understand why my Dad was so difficult all his life; he suffered terribly from depression and this came down right back from his Norfolk roots. He was an extremely difficult man and I have pretty obviously been following him, even though I have criticized him constantly, I am pretty much the same as him. If you have depression, or if you suffer from it, please don't keep it hidden. That's the worst thing you can do. After all, you deserve a life. You deserve to be recognised as a whole person. You don't deserve to be recognised as an illness. That's not the way to treat people. People with depression are often different from the "normal" but that's something to be celebrated and not to be criticised and lambasted.

Depressives – are we neurodivergent?

For what it's worth, yes I definitely think I am; there's definitely something which is quite different from the way I think than the way other people think. I can trace this right the way back to school. I did not have difficulty with many subjects but I was so bored with them. I had trouble with the music master especially. I just wanted to beat him up. I don't know whether that was a common feeling among pupils in my year group but I just disliked that man so much.

Yes, I was bored and could not concentrate, something so typical of ADHD students in the modern era. I enjoyed English and I enjoyed creative writing because I enjoyed expressing myself a lot and still do. Especially now that I have a speech defect and cannot express myself in conversation.

I noticed this inability to concentrate way back in 1980; I was on a course at Brooklands Technical College, I was doing communications RSA stage 2. However I would do my own thing throughout the lessons whether it was some other subject, or reading a book or a newspaper. I just would not participate in the lesson. The lady in charge of the course was going to report me to the principal. Somehow she did not and I passed that course and got the examination certificate. So I took it all in without participating in the course. That is something I regard as being neurodivergent. It was something I did not need and there was no need for the tutor to get uptight about it either.

That's the problem with contemporary education; it does not allow for anything different, or anyone different. I also recall that they said I was disruptive when I first started on the railways; that's because I did not like their bullying chief clerk when I worked at Hampton Court Station.

I was better off on my own. I ran my own booking office at Oxshott Station for three years after Hampton Court and no-one said anything to me.

I am different about falling in love. When I fall in love and the person rejects me, I don't lose my love for them simply because they do that. I am the only person I know who carries on caring for people who have rejected me. I suppose that's what makes me a good Christian. I can see the bigger picture. I don't stop loving people simply because of rejection and I don't carry hatred in my heart for them and think that they should have done something different. The only time I get hurt in that situation is if they are nasty to me and spiteful; then I will get upset. Otherwise I can keep on loving them without ever telling them. That's why I think I am different and perhaps neurodivergent.

I have lots of interests that would drive "normal" (neurotypical) people round the twist. I still have a love of buses and bus journeys and would still be able to find my way around London on a bus without even using a map. Come to think of it I could still find my way up to London without using a bus map, or timetables!

I am sometimes obsessive compulsive (OCD) which is a sign of being neurodivergent; I have dreadful dreams of hurting people with whom I have been in love. One such dream occurred in about 2000; I dreamed that a girl I was very much in love with had died. I dreamed that it was somehow my fault and that I had put too much pressure on her or had made demands on her. Fortunately this was only a dream and she was very much alive after I had my dream, so my love for her could not have been that bad.

I would always want to do a job my own way rather than "by the book!" They used to note that when I was in the Inland Revenue; they would send me on missions to other offices in other parts of the country and then that office would say that I had been paid too many expenses because I could make my way to London at the weekend. I would point out that my outstation was at least 40 miles from my home station and therefore I would be entitled to all the expenses. So therefore I gave the other office a cheque and went to the bank and cancelled it. I had a good grounding in the staff manual and I am afraid they gave up on that one. Most staff would have caved in but I am afraid not me. I am proud of my differences and not sorry to be different from others. I don't believe that people should be browbeaten and denigrated at work by rule-twisters.

With that particular department, they did not want to pay the bill for the additional staff member out of their budget; that's what that particular event turned out to be, even though they wanted me to work there. That's extremely hypocritical of them to want someone to work there for free, or try to get free labour from other offices by bucking the system. So my own senior principal inspector had to pay for it out of his own budget; that was an extremely bad experience and showed me what that government organisation was really all about at the time.

If I am not neurodivergent then all I can say is that I share a lot with neurodivergent and there is a growing body of opinion that would endorse my contention. I still say that I don't think or act the same way as others; I have a sister who has Aspergers and I just think or conclude that I am on the neurodivergent scale myself.

Depression - my personal journey - summary and conclusions

What I think could be done to stem the tide of childhood and adult depression in this country of ours is that, one must have the best parenting; it seems to me that a lot of us go into parenting with very little comprehension of what it actually involves, what we are dealing with here is the raising of a young life to be the best that he or she can be and that's just not possible if the parents are suffering from terrible mental illness and stress themselves.

We must provide for families, not cut their benefits. This is what is so important that if anyone decides to have more than two children then we cut their benefits. But I just don't see the difference between having two or three children. Every child born is a miracle in my book and thus we should not be making efforts to starve children out of their own homes.

Providing for families also means making provision for the best schools and the best housing that we can possibly muster. Making sure that we have the best teachers; there was some argument a while ago that maybe dinner ladies should be recruited to be teachers, such things are stuff and nonsense.

Get people into this worthy profession that can really teach and who have degrees with whom they can really impart knowledge. We must also take advantage of the private sector of education to provide facilities where and when they can and that would include providing scholarships to more children that they already do.

We must provide the best universities and teacher training establishments, not a system of old fogeys who can't teach, so they become lecturers and the people that we employ must be good lecturers.

We must stop seeing education as some kind of sausage machine and we must start treating children as individuals, not just as sheep who need to get through the sausage machine. We need to get to know the talents of our offspring so we can best guide them and put them on the right path.

We need to get more educated about what mental illness is; I was staggered to find out that that so many Irish people maintain that it is a person's personal fault if they suffer from mental illness. It is most definitely not and we must put the block on such erroneous thinking. Mental illness is a Cinderella service in our country and in others too and I would definitely want to put a lot of money into this service to bring it up to the level that it should be.

We must have the kind of society that is suitably educated and aware so that terrible things like the Horizon sub postmaster scandal do not happen; I was delighted to hear that Alan Bates was awarded a knighthood and he accepted it, that guy is a national hero and should really be appreciated as such.

 An adjunct to this is that we should not have a government that is so corrupt; this one has been the most corrupt since the days of Lloyd George. A government that is all in for themselves and their rich friends really should not be tolerated. I feel the winds of change are blowing in this respect and I hope and pray that we do have the right sort of government after 4th July 2024.

Overall, we must have more understanding of what mental illness is; I would really like the church to do more in this respect, we do an awful lot in providing aid and water and stuff for the developing countries but it would be helpful if our church, the RC church, we also to take an interest in mental health and to reach out to people who suffer depression and give them a message of hope and to pray for them. I am not saying that the RC church does not do this at present but I would really like it to do more of it.

I want everyone to do more to help mental illness and to be aware of it, the more the merrier, we must be the kind of society that becomes aware of people's troubles and not to turn them away and just think that the person is not worthy of attention. Everyone is worthy of attention.

That's my bill of rights and if we do get a new government on 04.07.2024 that is what I would want their mandate to be, to help and assist our children to grow up in a sane world, not an insane one full of wars and troubles. Finally, I would hope and pray that some of my ideas in these closing paragraphs are taken on. Thank you for reading thus far and I sincerely hope that you have enjoyed this book.

Book dedication:-

This work is dedicated to my friend MF who has been an inspiration.